NEW YORK STATE GRADE 3 ELEMENTARY-LEVEL ENGLISH LANGUAGE ARTS TEST

Janet A. Gallant, M.Ed.

BARRON'S

About the Author

Janet Gallant is currently the Kindergarten and Primary School Principal in Hudson Falls, New York. She has taught third grade at Queensbury Elementary School in Queensbury, New York, where she also participated in curriculum development. She was an assistant professor of education at the College of St. Joseph in Rutland, Vermont. This is her first book for Barron's.

Dedication

To my husband, Kevin, thank you for your endless encouragement and support. To my daughter, Kate, your accomplishments in the pool are an inspiration to me. Thank you for your patience throughout this endeavor. To my son, Zachary, and his son, Aaden, good luck to both of you. Aaden, you will take your first state test in 2009. To my students who have contributed the stories for the practice tests, thank you. I am proud of all of you. And to a special friend, Emily Singer, you have taught me more than you will ever know.

Janet Gallant

All inquiries should be addressed to:
Barron's Educational Series, Inc.
250 Wireless Boulevard
Hauppauge, NY 11788
www.barronseduc.com

ISBN-13: 978-0-7641-4081-5
ISBN-10: 0-7641-4081-7
ISSN: 1942-0145

Printed in the United States of America
9 8 7 6 5 4 3 2 1

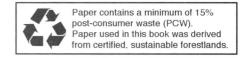

Paper contains a minimum of 15% post-consumer waste (PCW). Paper used in this book was derived from certified, sustainable forestlands.

Contents

INTRODUCTION FOR STUDENTS, PARENTS, AND TEACHERS

STUDENTS

Have you heard the buzz about the state test you will be taking in third grade? Third grade is the year you will take your first New York State English Language Arts (ELA) Test. Every third-grade student in New York State will take this test in January. The test will measure how well you are using the reading and writing skills you are being taught in school.

LEARNING TO READ

Your teachers have been teaching you to read since you entered kindergarten. First, you learned the names of the letters. Then you learned the sounds to think about when you read the letters. Next, you learned to read words. Have you noticed that now, in third grade, many words are easy to read? In fact, you hardly think about the letters as you read many words.

Try this. Read the following sentences.

I like to run. I like to jump. I like to skip. Do you like to run and jump and skip?

Did you notice that you did not have to think about the letters and sounds as you read the words? That's because you have seen these words so many times that you can read the whole words quickly.

READING TO LEARN

When you don't have to think about reading the words, you can think more about the meaning of the story. You can learn new information by reading. This is what your teacher calls reading comprehension. You are learning new skills and strategies to help you understand what you read.

LEARNING NEW SKILLS

Learning anything new takes practice. Lots of it! When you practice, new skills become more automatic. You use them without thinking about them. Picture an athlete in your mind. Athletes can make a sport look very easy. That is the result of a lot of practice.

Have you ever watched an Olympic swimmer? They dive in and swim as fast as they can to the end of the pool, do a flip turn, and then swim back to the other end of the pool—over and over again until the race is finished. A flip turn is like a summersault under water. The turns have to be fast if the swimmer wants to win the race.

My daughter, Kate, is a competitive swimmer. I remember when she first learned to do a flip turn. She had to practice flip turns many times. She would come home after practice and say:

"I hate flip turns. I hate flip turns. I hate flip turns!"

Kate did not like flip turns because they were hard to learn. She had to practice many new things. Her hands had to be in just the right place. Her legs had to tuck close to her body before she could begin to curl them over her head. She had to touch the wall of the pool in a special way. Her feet had to be in just the right place. Then she had to bend her knees, push off the wall, roll back into her stroke, and swim fast. There was so much to think about at the same time!

Kate's swim coach knew that she could not be thinking about all this and swim fast. So, he made her practice flip turns over and over. After all that practice her body learned what to do. The hard work and practice paid off! Now Kate's flip turns are fast, and she has won many races.

READING COMPREHENSION

Have you ever thought about reading as a new skill? Just as in learning to do a flip turn, you have to think about many things at one time.

When you read, you have to think about the words, sentences, and paragraphs. You have to think about where and when the story takes place. You have to think about the characters and their feelings. You also have to think about the main idea of the story.

When you put all this thinking together, you understand the meaning of the story you are reading.

USING WHAT YOU HAVE LEARNED

Remember, learning something new takes practice. This book was written to help you prepare for your first New York State English Language Arts Test. This book will guide your thinking as you practice.
Here is what you will find in this book.

1. A separate chapter for each section of the ELA test
2. Instruction to guide your thinking as you practice
3. An opportunity to test your skills in each chapter
4. Two complete practice tests with detailed answers
5. Charts to help you remember the language of the test
6. Charts to help you remember the strategies you will use as you practice.

WORK WITH A COACH

The greatest athletes have a coach to help them learn new skills. Ask a family member to coach you and help you with the guided practice in this book.

WHAT TO EXPECT ON THE STATE ASSESSMENT TEST

There are three parts to the ELA test. You will take the test in two sessions. Here is a chart that shows you what each session will be like.

Session	Skills Tested	Types of Questions	Time
Day 1, Book 1	• Reading comprehension	• Multiple choice • Constructed response	50 minutes
Day 2, Book 2	• Listening comprehension • Writing	• Multiple choice • Constructed response • Editing paragraph	60 minutes

Book 1 will test your reading comprehension. You will read four short passages. Then you will answer a few questions about each one.

Book 2 has two parts. Part 1 will test how well you learn new information when you listen to a story. You will hear the story two times before you answer the questions.

Book 2 will also measure your use of basic writing skills. You will read a short paragraph and correct mistakes in punctuation.

GRAPHICS AND CHARTS

Graphics are used in this book to help guide your thinking. You will find charts in the first four chapters to help you remember the thinking process you will use while you read and answer the comprehension questions. There is a glossary at the back of the book to help you remember the words and concepts that you will see on the ELA test.

LANGUAGE OF THE TEST

This book was written to help you prepare for the state ELA test. The stories and questions in this book are similar to those on the state test. The guided practice and the charts in this book will help you get ready for the test.

WHAT GOOD READERS DO AND THINK

Good readers think about the story before they start reading. When you see this symbol, you will be told what to think about before you start to read and answer the questions.

ANSWERING THE QUESTIONS

1. Sometimes the author includes all the important details in the story. The reader can find the correct answers to some questions by looking at the words the author has written in the story.
2. Sometimes the author provides important information in the text but the words for the answer are not written in the text. The reader has to connect what they know and what the author has said to select or write the correct answer.

ATTENTION

This symbol lets you know that there is something important to notice and remember.

CHARTS

You will find charts in Chapters 1–4 that will help you remember the new words and strategies to use as you read. These strategies will help you become a better reader. They will also help you on the state ELA test.

BEFORE YOU START

Remember the swimmer, the flip turns, and the coach. Kate could not learn to do flip turns by herself. She needed a coach to guide her as she practiced new skills.

Like Kate, you are practicing new skills. You may need someone to help you practice and prepare for the state ELA test.

Ask a parent or another family member to help you. Let them read the next section. After that, you can work together and prepare for your first New York State English Language Arts Test.

PARENTS

In third grade your child will take the New York State English Language Arts Test. This is the first of many state assessment tests that your child will take as they continue through their public education. The Grade 3 ELA Test will measure how well your child is using the reading, writing, and listening skills they have been taught in grades K–3.

PURPOSE OF THE NEW YORK STATE ENGLISH LANGUAGE ARTS TEST

The Grade 3 ELA Test meets the requirements of the No Child Left Behind Act (2001). Under the NCLB act, all states are required to establish state academic standards and learning objectives. Each state must also develop a testing system for grades 3–8. These tests will measure the school's effectiveness in delivering instruction that supports the academic achievement of its students.

The Grade 3 ELA Test is developed to measure how well students apply grade-level reading, writing, and listening skills as determined to be appropriate by the New York State Learning Standards.

OVERVIEW OF THE TEST

The test will be administered in two sessions. The chart below outlines each day of the test.

Session	Skills Tested	Types of Questions	Time
Day 1, Book 1	• Reading comprehension 4 reading passages	• 20 Multiple choice • 1 Constructed response (short response)	10 minutes Directions 40 minutes Student reading and response
Day 2, Book 2	• Listening comprehension • Writing	• Multiple choice • Constructed response • Editing paragraph	15 minutes Directions and listening 35 minutes Student response

LANGUAGE AND SKILLS OF THE TEST

To be successful on the ELA test, your child will use the skills and strategies they have been learning in school. A brief summary follows.

Reading comprehension:

■ Read and understand fiction and nonfiction texts
■ Read for the main idea and the details
■ Locate important information in the text
■ Draw conclusions and inferences using what they know and the information stated in the text
■ Answer multiple-choice and short written-response questions.

Listening comprehension:

- Listen to a story for understanding and recall
- Listen for the main ideas and details
- Take notes to help recall important information
- Answer multiple-choice and short written-response questions.

Writing / editing passage:

- Edit a brief paragraph
- Apply their knowledge of capitalization and punctuation rules.

TESTING ACCOMMODATIONS FOR STUDENTS WITH SPECIAL NEEDS

Test accommodations are designated by the New York State Department of Education. Students with an Individualized Education Program (IEP) may have extended time to complete the test if that accommodation is approved by the district's Committee on Special Education. There are few other accommodations provided for the state assessment test. If your child has an IEP, you should check with the district's special education director for information regarding their eligibility for testing accommodations.

SCORING THE ELA TEST

The New York State Department of Education provides training to all scorers to ensure that all tests across the state are scored in a uniform manner. This training includes an overview of high-quality responses for each question requiring a written response. The New York State Department of Education has established specific guidelines to ensure equity in scoring all tests across the state. A rubric is provided by the state to score each written response. A sample scoring rubric is provided in Appendix 3 of this book.

UNDERSTANDING THE TEST RESULTS

The results of the ELA test are usually released in the spring. NCLB requires that districts provide the public with information about the school's performance. Published results do not include individual student test results.

The school district will provide a Parent Report that details your child's individual results. A brief summary of the information on this report is provided in an appendix of this book. However, the commonly discussed score is the level of performance. This is a score of 1, 2, 3, or 4. It is an estimation of your child's achievement based only on the results of the ELA assessment test. The chart below explains the implications of level of performance scores.

Score	Descriptor	Implication
4	Student performance demonstrates a thorough understanding of the ELA standards expected at this grade level.	Meets standards.
3	Student performance demonstrates an understanding of the ELA standards expected at this grade level.	
2	Student performance demonstrates a partial understanding of the ELA standards expected at this grade level.	Does not meet standards. Additional instruction and intervention services will be needed.
1	Student performance does not demonstrate an understanding of the ELA standards expected at this grade level.	

WHAT GOOD READERS THINK AND DO

Reading is an active but invisible processing of information, thoughts, and ideas. When a child listens to an experienced reader read out loud, the process of reading and comprehension appears to be automatic. The ease with which an experienced reader can read is the result of effective instruction and time spent practicing.

Your child is learning and developing the skills and strategies used by effective readers. In brief, those skills and strategies include:

Identify details
Identify the sequence of events
Connect cause and effect
Determine the main idea
Make inferences and predictions
Use sensory images
Question the text
Synthesize and extend
Monitor comprehension
Problem-solve

GUIDED PRACTICE AND TEST YOUR SKILLS

This book was written to help your child learn and practice the skills and strategies used by proficient readers. Each of the **guided practice** chapters ends with a **Test Your Skills** question set. The answers for the guided practice follow each question. This immediate feedback will help your child learn how to think like a good reader. The answers to the Test Your Skills questions can be found in the answer key at the back of the book. This provides an opportunity for independent practice of the skills taught in the chapter.

SUGGESTIONS FOR SUPPORTING DEVELOPING READERS

Think out loud as you read to your child. The guided practice in this book does just that. This book provides a detailed explanation of the thinking process used to understand each text and the questions that follow each reading and listening passage.

Because research has repeatedly shown that parental involvement is crucial to student success, this book was developed in a format that includes an opportunity for you to provide guided assistance for your child.

1. **What Good Readers Do and Think:** This section provides information for the developing reader to think about before they begin to read. This may activate their background knowledge on the topic. Help your child understand the thought process explained in this section.

2 **Question and Answer Strategies:** This section provides information to help the developing reader understand the question and the thinking process for selecting or developing the correct answer. Help your child understand the benefits of the thinking process described in this section.

3. **Attention:** In this book, graphics are used to call the reader's attention to an important word or concept that will help the reader understand the language on the New York State ELA Test. Help focus your child's attention on the key words used on the ELA test.

4. **Charts:** Several charts are included in this book to help your child remember important information presented in this book and in their classroom reading instruction. The information presented in this book will benefit your child well beyond the New York State ELA Test experience.

GUIDED ASSISTANCE

A child could complete the guided practices in this book independently; however, your participation may provide the level of support necessary for a developing reader.

APPENDICES

There are appendices in this book that provide additional information pertinent to the topics presented in this brief introduction.

BEYOND THIS BOOK

The practice provided by this book may help your child's performance on the New York State ELA Test. The guided and independent practice provided in this book will help your child develop the skills used by effective and efficient readers. More importantly, however, these are the skills and strategies that will help your child become a successful lifelong learner.

TEACHERS

You have been given the daunting task of preparing young children for their first New York State English Language Arts Test. As a curriculum and standards leader, I have developed materials for and assisted grade 3 teachers as they prepared their students for the state ELA assessment. This book is a result of my research and collaboration with many highly qualified third-grade teachers.

This book was designed to provide instruction and practice in the skills and strategies used by proficient readers. The passages and tasks were developed to replicate the Grade 3 ELA Test. The guided practice includes detailed explanations that direct the reader in applying the cognitive reading strategies recommended by prominent researchers in the field of reading comprehension. Each of the guided practice chapters ends with a **Test Your Skills** independent practice. The answers to these questions can be found in the answer key at the back of the book.

There are several charts in Chapters 1–4. They are designed to assist the students using this book. However, because they are based on current research in the field of reading comprehension, they can also be used to support the instruction children are receiving in your classroom. While the words I use may not exactly match the words used in your classroom, the principles supporting the strategies should be the same.

It is my hope that this book can be a helpful resource to you, your students, and their parents or guardians as you work together to achieve successful student performance on the state assessment test.

READING COMPREHENSION AND MULTIPLE-CHOICE QUESTIONS

It is important to remember that most of the points you can earn on the New York State ELA Test will come from answering the multiple-choice questions correctly. Take your time reading the passages and the guided practice that follows each question. The guide will explain the thinking process a reader uses to answer the question.

GOOD READERS THINK WHILE THEY READ

A good reader knows that there are different strategies to help them understand the text they are reading. Good readers think about the text and ask themselves questions as they read to help them understand the meaning of the text. A good reader also uses strategies to help them understand each question before selecting the best answer to the question.

There are charts at the end of this chapter that will help you remember the strategies to use while you are reading.

GUIDED PRACTICE AND TEST YOUR SKILLS

This chapter provides instruction and practice in answering multiple-choice questions. There are five reading passages followed by multiple-choice questions.

The first four passages include guided practice. First, read the passage. Next, read the question and select your answer. Then, check to see if you have selected the correct answer. Finally, read the hints and explanations that will help you think like a good reader.

The last reading passage will Test Your Skills. The answers are not included in this chapter. First, read the passage and answer the multiple-choice questions. Then, look at the answer key at the back of the book to find out if you selected the correct answer.

GUIDED PRACTICE 1

The first passage is a narrative. A **narrative** can be fiction or nonfiction. A narrative may include information that will help the reader understand the characters' feelings. This is important to remember. The reader can learn a lot about the story by understanding the characters' feelings.

Before you start…take a look at what good readers do and think about when they read a narrative.

WHAT GOOD READERS DO AND THINK

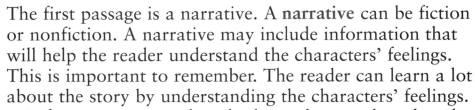

Remember—a narrative tells a story. Think about the characters and events as you read the story.

Read the title and look at the pictures. **Swim to Win**
This could be about a race.
Read the first sentence. **When my daughter was 14 she swam on a high school swim team.**
Have you ever wanted to win something?
How would you feel if you were in her place?
Focus your thinking.
This story is about a high school sport. Focus on the details of the story and the feelings of the characters.

Okay, you are ready to begin. The questions include the language that you will see on the state test.

Directions:

Read this story. Then answer questions 1–4.

Swim to Win

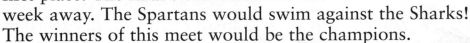

When Kate was 14 she swam on a high school swim team. Kate's team, the Spartans, wanted to win the championship. Their rival team, the Sharks, also wanted to win the championship. With one meet left in the season, the Spartans and Sharks were in a tie for first place. The final swim meet was one week away. The Spartans would swim against the Sharks! The winners of this meet would be the champions.

The Sharks' coach wanted his team to win. The Sharks practiced twice a day. They practiced in the morning and in the afternoon. The Spartans' coach wanted his team to win. The Spartans practiced twice a day. They practiced after school, took a break, and practiced again in the evening.

The day of the final swim meet was here. Both teams were ready. The crowd cheered as each girl swam as fast as she could. When the meet was over the Spartans went home very happy!

1. What is this story **mostly** about?
    A. Kate swam on a high school swim team.
    B. Two fast high school swim teams.
    C. Two high school swim teams that wanted to win the championship.
    D. Two swim teams that had to practice two times a day.

The correct answer is **C**. This passage is **mostly** about two teams that wanted to win a championship. Think about the meaning of the entire story to answer this question.

Hint: The choices **A**, **B**, and **D** are details that support the main idea, but they are not the *main idea.*

Did you notice…?
The key words guide the reader's thinking.

2. What did **both** coaches do to get their team ready for the final swim meet?
    A. Practice in the morning.
    B. Practice two times a day.
    C. Rest the team so they will be ready to swim.
    D. Practice twice in the afternoon

The correct answer is **B**. The key word in this question is "both." The words that answer this question are in the story.

Hint: Pay attention to the key word in the question.

Choices **A** and **D** are true of **one** coach, not both coaches. Choice **C** did not happen in this story.

Did you notice…?
To answer this question the reader has to think about vocabulary. The word "twice" has the same meaning as "two."

3. Read this line from the story.

    Their rival team, the Sharks, also wanted to win the championship.

    The word "rival" **most likely** means
    A. friendship.
    B. contest.
    C. winning.
    D. competitor.

The correct answer is **D**. This is another vocabulary question. The key phrase **most likely** means help the reader to know that the correct answer is a **synonym**—a word that has a meaning close to "rival."

Hint: There is a process of thinking used to answer this question.

Look back at the sentence in the story.
Think about the main idea of the paragraph.

(Two teams want to win—that means they are competing.)

Which word could be used in the sentence and have the same meaning?

You **compete** with a **competitor**, so...

their competitors, the Sharks, also want to win the division championship.

Did you follow this thinking?
There could be questions like this on the New York State ELA Test.

4. Why did the Spartan team go home happy?
   A. They won the swim meet and the championship.
   B. They were glad the season was over.
   C. They liked to practice twice a day.
   D. They lost the swim meet.

The correct answer is **A**. For this question the reader must think about what the author wrote and what they already know or feel. The author never told the reader why the Spartans were happy. But the author did provide clues to help answer this question.

Hint: Think about the characters' feelings.

The Spartans and Sharks both wanted to win the championship.

Have you ever wanted to win something?

How would you feel if you won?

The author *told* the reader the Spartans went home happy.

The reader can connect with the Spartans' feelings and actions.

The Spartans were happy because they won the championship.

Did you notice…

In this question the first choice was correct. Don't be fooled. Sometimes the first choice seems like the correct answer. Sometimes there is a more complete answer in another choice.

Read all the choices before selecting the correct answer.

That was a lot of thinking for four questions! This type of thinking may be new to you. Remember, you have to think a lot about what you are doing when you learn something new. With practice, this thinking will become more automatic. So…keep practicing.

GUIDED PRACTICE 2

The second passage is a **nonfiction article**. A passage like this could be found in a science textbook. A nonfiction article includes many details about the topic. These details will help the reader answer the multiple-choice questions.

Some of the words used in a nonfiction article may be new to the reader. The information in a nonfiction article will explain the new words.

Before you start…take a look at what good readers do and think about when they read a nonfiction article.

WHAT GOOD READERS DO AND THINK

Remember—nonfiction is about facts and information. Look for new words and new information as you read.

Read the title. Look at the pictures and diagrams.

A Frog's Life

The main topic will be the life of a frog. Readers should think about what they already know about the life of a frog.

Look for headings in the article before reading the article.

Look for bold print headings

Life Begins in an Egg

This will tell about a frog's life starting as an egg.

The Tadpole Begins to Change

This will tell about the changes in the life of a tadpole.

Hint: The paragraphs before the first heading may be an introduction to grab the reader's attention. The important topic details may start *after* the first heading.

Focus your thinking.

Look for facts and details as you read. Underline the details so it will be easy to find them again to answer detail questions. Focus on the order of changes as they are explained.

You are ready for another practice. The questions include the language that you will see on the state test.

Directions:

Read this story. Then answer questions 5–10.

A Frog's Life

When you were born, your family and friends saw how much you looked like your mother or your father. Perhaps your eyes were the same shape as your dad's. Or maybe your chin looked just like your mom's. Well, no one ever said those things about a baby frog. A baby frog does not look anything like an adult frog. In fact, baby frogs are not even called frogs! They are called tadpoles.

Adult frogs have long hind legs and short bodies. They do not have tails. Frogs have protruding eyes that bulge out from their heads. They also have webbed feet. This is not what they looked like when they were born.

Life Begins in an Egg

Frogs lay their eggs in water or wet places. The eggs are in a jellylike substance and clump together. This large clump of eggs is called frog spawn. Some frogs can lay more than 1,000 eggs! Only a few of the eggs will survive to grow into adult frogs.

Life for a frog begins when a single cell inside the egg begins to split. Each surviving egg is now called an embryo. The life that is now growing in the egg looks like a tadpole. In three weeks the tadpole will hatch with gills, a mouth, and a tail.

The Tadpole Begins to Change

In five weeks the tadpole begins another cycle of change. First, it starts to grow legs. Next, the lungs begin to develop. The front legs will begin to grow before the tail disappears. The tadpole is now called a froglet. It looks like a tiny frog with a tail! Just a few more weeks and the cycle will be complete. Sixteen weeks after hatching, the frog has gone through a complete growth cycle.

Now the baby looks like its mother and father!

5. According to this article frogs lay their eggs in
   A. logs.
   B. ponds.
   C. water or wet places.
   D. underground.

The correct answer is C. This question asks for a detail from the story. The author used the words in the article that will answer this question. Look back at the article for the details.

Did you notice...?
   The second choice sounds correct.
   Hint: The key words in this question are **according to this article**. This question is asking for facts the author has included in the passage. The author did not mention a pond. Select the answer that includes the facts the author stated in the article.

6. Read this sentence from the article.

> Frogs have protruding eyes that bulge out from their heads.

This sentence tells you that
A. a frog has large eyes.
B. a frog has eyes on the top of its head.
C. a frog has green eyes.
D. a frog has eyes that stick out above its head.

The correct answer is D. The author included information to answer this question *but* the reader had to think about two words in this sentence to select the correct answer. Choices A and B are true *but* do not include the best details to answer the question.

Hint: This question is a vocabulary question. The words "protrude" and "bulge" are important in the sentence. Both words mean *to stick out.*

Did you notice…?

The author has included a picture of a frog with this article. The picture includes details to help answer this question! Look at the frog's eyes in the picture. They are large. They are on the top of its head. But, did you notice that the eyes stick out above its head?

Remember—a nonfiction article includes information to help the reader learn new vocabulary.

You may find questions like this on the New York State ELA Test.

7. The chart below shows details from the article.

Legs begin to grow.		The tadpole is now a froglet.	The frog's growth cycle is complete.

According to this article, which sentence belongs in the empty box?
A. The eggs are laid in water.
B. The lungs begin to develop.
C. The cells begin to split.
D. The tail falls off.

The correct answer is **B.**
  Hint: To answer this question look at the order of *events in this article.*

Did you notice…?
  The **bold print headings** organize information in a non-fiction article. Readers can use the headings to help them find the details to answer to this question.
  Here's how:

  Life Begins in an Egg: This section explains the changes that happen while the baby frog is in the egg.
  The Tadpole Begins to Change: This section explains the changes after the baby frog becomes a tadpole.
  Next, look at the first box in this question. *Legs begin to grow.*
  Think: Do the legs grow while the frog is in the egg or when the frog is a tadpole?
  Now: Go back and read the tadpole section again. The words for the answer are written in the article.
  The lungs begin to develop **after** the legs begin to grow.

  Did you follow that thinking?
  There may be questions like this on the New York State ELA Test.

8. The author most likely wrote this article to
   A. Tell you what a tadpole looks like.
   B. Describe the life cycle of a frog.
   C. Explain the words "frog spawn."
   D. Tell you that a baby frog does not look like an adult frog.

The correct answer is B. This question asks the *author's purpose* for writing this article. More than one choice may look correct. Think about all the information the author has included in this article. The author wrote this article to describe the life cycle of a frog.

Hint: There is a process of thinking used to answer this question.
Think about:

What is the most important information in this article?
Look at the bold print headings.
   This article describes the life cycle of a frog.

The author included an introduction to grab the reader's attention.

> It is fun to think that babies look like their parents when they are born. It is interesting to think that a baby frog does not look at all like its parents when it is born.

Be careful! This is only an introduction. This is not the reason the author wrote this article.

Look at why the other choices are not the correct answer.
   A. The article explains more than what a tadpole looks like. This answer sounds correct, but the reader should read all the choices before selecting the answer.

C. The author explains what "frog spawn" means to help the reader understand the main idea of this article.

D. There was an introduction to grab the reader's attention. The main idea and important details begin *after* the introduction.

There could be a question like this on the state ELA test.

9. Read this sentence from the article.

> Only a few of the eggs will survive to grow into adult frogs.

This **most likely** means

A. The adult frog laid too many eggs.

B. Many eggs will be eaten by predators.

C. Some eggs will remain as tadpoles.

D. The frog spawn was too crowded.

The correct answer is **B**. The author did not explain this statement. The reader has to think about what they know and the details in this article. The reader will draw a conclusion to answer this question.

Did you notice...?

Thinking about science will help you answer this question. The word predator is a science vocabulary word. A predator is an animal, or organism, that kills for food. In nature it is likely that there are animals that will eat the frog eggs.

Hint: This question did *not* have the words according to this article. The answer to this question may not be stated in the article. The reader must draw a logical conclusion to select the correct answer.

10. Which sentence from this article is **not a fact**?
- **A.** The large clump of eggs is called a frog spawn.
- **B.** A surviving egg is called an embryo
- **C.** A baby frog develops lungs when it is a tadpole.
- **D.** Maybe your chin looked like your mom's.

The correct answer is D. The key words in this question are **not a fact**.

Hint: Here's the thinking for this question.

- A **fact** is something that is known to be true.
- Choices A and B are science vocabulary words. Each statement is a **fact**.
- Choice C is known to be true and is a **fact**.

Now, you have read two passages and answered 10 questions. You are practicing the thinking process you will use on the state exam. Good for you!

GUIDED PRACTICE 3

The next passage is a poem. It is quite likely that there will be a poem to read on the state test. Poetry often uses **figurative language** to create images for the reader. There may be questions on the test that ask the reader to explain the meaning of the figurative language used in the poem.

Before you start ... look at what good readers do and think when they read poetry.

WHAT GOOD READERS DO AND THINK

Remember—use your senses to help you understand figurative language.

Read the title and look at the pictures. The Day Trip
This poem could be about traveling to a special place.
Read the poem for the first time.
What is the main idea?
Focus your attention on the characters and the setting.
Look for **figurative language**.
Read the poem again.
Think about the meaning of the figurative language.
What words did the poet use to help the reader see the images described? What words were used to help the reader feel what the poet felt?

Directions:

Read the poem. Then answer questions 11–16.

The Day Trip

We took the train to the city today,
    Just to see what we might see.
The sights and sounds, the people and places,
    Were such a wonder to me!

I traveled with Mom—she's been here before,
    So she knew just what to do.
Stand at the corner and hail a cab,
    To take us to the Bronx Zoo!

Tigers and monkeys, gorillas and bats,
    Giraffes as tall as a cloud.
I jumped at a sound I thought was thunder.
    Lions can roar very loud!

After the zoo—in a taxi again,
  To join a friend for a show.
We drove through the streets so crowded with cars,
  All horns would constantly blow!

We entered the theater at five o'clock,
  The music began to play.
Colorful costumes and wonderful songs,
  This is a wonderful day!

Later that night as we rode the train home,
  I thanked my mom for the trip.
If you have a chance to travel one day,
  The city would be my tip!

11. What is this poem **mostly** about?
    A. a train ride
    B. the Bronx Zoo
    C. a trip to the city
    D. watching a show

The correct answer is C. The key words in this question are **mostly about**. This is a main idea question. The poet gives the reader all the information to answer this question, <u>but</u> the reader has to put the information together to understand the main idea.

  Hint: Choices A, B, and D are details that support the main idea.

12. What would be another good title for this poem?
    A. My Train Ride
    B. The Bronx Zoo
    C. My First Trip to the City
    D. Meeting a Friend

The correct answer is C.

Did you notice...?
This is another way to ask for the main idea of this poem. Choice **C** is the correct answer because the other choices are the supporting details that describe the trip to the city.

Hint: The title of a passage most often gives a clue about the main idea.

13. The person telling the story in this poem **most likely**
 A. enjoyed the train ride.
 B. had never been to the city before.
 C. was tired after the trip.
 D. was a very young child.

The correct answer is **B**.
Hint: To answer this question the reader must think about what the author says in this poem. The reader must draw a conclusion using the information they learn from the author.
 Follow this thinking:

> The poem did not tell how the person felt about the train ride.
> The sights and sounds of the city were a *wonder* to this traveler. The mother was on this trip because she had been to the city before and knew what to do.
> The person telling the story may have been tired after the trip, but the poem did not say that.
> The person traveled with his or her mother, so it was a child. However, the poem gave you no clues about the child's age.

 So ... the **most likely** answer is **B**. The **wonder** suggests that these sights are new.

Did you follow this thinking?
 There may be a question like this on the New York State ELA Test.

14. Read this line from the poem.

Giraffes as tall as a cloud.

The poet wrote this line so the reader would

A. look up at the sky.

B. see a white giraffe.

C. know it was a cloudy day.

D. see a very tall giraffe.

The correct answer is D. This is an example of figurative language. The poet used a simile to compare two unlike things.

Hint: Figurative language is used to create a strong image in the reader's mind.

Follow this thinking:

Giraffes are tall.

Clouds are high in the sky.

You have to look up really high to see clouds.

The poet wanted the reader to know that they would have to look up really high to see the top of the giraffe.

So … the poet wanted the reader to see a very tall giraffe!

15. Read the last line of this poem.

The city would be my tip!

In this poem the word "tip" means

A. money you give to a waitress.

B. a new idea.

C. the sharp end of a pencil.

D. advice.

The correct answer is D.

Did you notice…?

This is a vocabulary question. The reader must use what they know about the word "tip" and connect it to the meaning of this poem.

Hint: The word "tip" has more than one meaning. Choices **A** and **C** could be correct *if* you miss the key words: in this poem.

Did you notice…?
 The key words focus attention on the meaning of the word "tip" as it is used in *this* poem.

16. Read the chart below.

My Trip to the City
Ride a train to the city.
Enter the theater at five o'clock.

Which phrase best completes the chart?
A. Thank Mom for the trip.
B. Saw colorful costumes.
C. Saw a large giraffe at the zoo.
D. Rode the train home.

The correct answer is **C**.
 Hint: Think about the order of events in this story. Go back and read the details again before selecting the answer.

Did you notice…?
 Seeing the giraffe is the only event that happened **after** the train ride *and* **before** entering the theater.

You are almost finished with the multiple-choice guided practice. You are thinking like a good reader.

GUIDED PRACTICE 4

The last passage is a story with dialogue. A story can be told by the words the characters speak.

Before you start … look at what good readers do and think when they read a story with a lot of dialogue.

WHAT GOOD READERS DO AND THINK

Remember—the words inside the quotation marks are the words the character is saying.

Read the title and look at the pictures. **Winter Vacation** This could be about planning a vacation, going on a vacation, or a memory of a past vacation.

Follow the characters' conversation.
Watch where the quotation marks start and stop.

Focus on the characters' feelings.
Do the characters use words that show strong feelings and emotions?

Focus on the words the author uses to help the reader understand how the characters feel.
Look for word choices such as:

John **whispered,** "I am hungry."

John **cried,** "I am hungry."

John **shouted,** "I am hungry!"

You are ready for the last multiple-choice guided practice.

Directions:

Read this story about a winter vacation. Then answer questions 17–20.

Winter Vacation

"Wow, can you believe our winter vacation starts next week?"

"I know, Jim. You and your sister will have two weeks of winter fun," said Dad.

"I remember the fun you and Susan had last year," said Mom as she passed the carrots to Jim.

Susan started to laugh. "Hey, Dad. Do you remember when you and Mom tried to ride down the steepest hill together on the toboggan?"

"I sure remember!" said Jim. "I laughed so hard I fell down."

"But not as hard as I did," said Dad. "It's a good thing I was wearing my snowsuit."

Mom was remembering Dad rolling down the hill next to her. She was laughing when she said, "Let's have a different kind of fun this vacation."

17. According to this story, the winter vacation will begin
   A. in one week.
   B. in two weeks.
   C. in December.
   D. the next day.

The answer is **A.** This is a detail from the story. The character **tells** you in the first sentence.

Hint: Focus on the important words in this question. The question asks when the vacation will **begin**.

18. The author **most likely** wrote this story to
   A. remind the reader that the winter vacation will start soon.
   B. tell you that Susan and Jim will go on a vacation soon.
   C. tell you about a family dinner.
   D. share a memory from a past winter vacation.

The correct answer is **D**. The key words most likely focus the reader's attention on the *author's purpose* for writing this story. The characters in this story are talking about a memory from a past winter vacation.

Did you notice...?
   The information in choices **A**, **B**, and **C** are mentioned in this story but are *not* the main event.
   Hint: Try this!

   Create a picture in your mind about this story: Are you **most likely** to picture a family at a dinner table or Mom and Dad falling off a toboggan while sliding down a steep hill? **You most likely saw Mom and Dad falling off the toboggan.** This is a memory from a past vacation.

19. Read this sentence from the story.

> "Do you remember when you and Mom tried to ride down the steepest hill together on the toboggan?"

   A toboggan is **most likely**
   A. a large set of skis.
   B. ice skates.
   C. a sled.
   D. water skis.

The correct answer is **C**. This is a vocabulary question.

Hint: Follow this thinking.

Think about the setting of the main event in this story.

A memory of an event from a past winter vacation.

It is not likely that Mom and Dad went down a hill together on one set of skis or ice skates. It is not likely that Dad wore a snowsuit to water ski.

Use the picture included with this story to help answer this question.

20. The sentence that best describes the family in this story is:

    A. They are a family with seven children.

    B. They are a family that enjoys winter vacations.

    C. They are a family that does not like winter vacations.

    D. They are a family that does not like adventure.

The correct answer is **B**. The dialogue in this story helps the reader understand the family.

Did you notice…?

There were only two children talking in this story.

The family laughed at the memory of their past winter vacation.

The family is planning to take another winter vacation.

Riding a toboggan down a steep hill *is* an adventure.

TEST YOUR SKILLS

Directions:

Read the poem. Then answer questions 1–4.

Baby Sister

My sister learned to walk today,
   She took a step or two.
"That's great," I said, "Let's go out and play."
   Mom said, "Wait a day or two."

My sister walked and then she fell down,
   Her diapers softened the fall.
I guess Mom's right, she's up and she's down,
   Not ready to play at all.

My sister will need lots of practice,
   To be steady on her feet.
I'd really like to wait for you, Sis,
   But for now, I'll run with Pete!

1. The baby in this poem is learning to
    A. walk.
    B. play ball.
    C. play outside.
    D. talk.

2. Read this line from the poem:

    Her diapers softened the fall

    This line most likely means
    A. the baby cried when she fell.
    B. the baby did not get hurt when she fell.
    C. the heavy diaper made her fall.
    D. the diaper came off when the baby fell.

3. In this poem, the word "steady" means
   A. clumsy.
   B. unstable.
   C. shaky.
   D. balanced.

4. The person telling this story played with Pete now because
   A. Pete was a good friend.
   B. he did not want to play with his sister.
   C. the sister was not ready to run.
   D. the baby fell and was crying.

Answers are on page 153.

Congratulations! You have finished the multiple-choice practice.

The following charts summarize what you learned in this chapter, and can help you remember the strategies that good readers use every time they read.

CHART 1: UNDERSTANDING TYPES OF PASSAGES

Nonfiction		
Genre	Features of the Genre	Strategies
Informational text: Article	■ Provides factual information ■ Text is organized (text structure) to help readers understand the information ■ May contain graphic organizers such as photographs, charts, and diagrams to help the reader understand the topic ■ Bold headings tell the reader the topic of each section in the text ■ New vocabulary words are explained directly or through the use of context clues	■ Use the text structure to help you organize your thinking ■ Read the headings carefully ■ Use the information included in the graphic organizers ■ Underline the important information and details as you read ■ Look for similes that may help you compare new information to something more familiar to you ■ Use the clues the author provides to learn the new words in the text

Informational text: How-to	▪ Information presented in the order it must occur ▪ Cue words include: first, second, third, next, last, finally	▪ Follow the order presented in the text ▪ Do not leave out steps in the process when you recall information ▪ Look for cue words to follow the order of events ▪ Answer questions in the proper order of events
Personal narratives	▪ The author is recalling an event that really happened ▪ The setting and characters are real ▪ The author's purpose is usually to share a memory with the reader ▪ The characters' feelings are important and often provide the reader with important information to help them understand and appreciate the author's memory	▪ Pay attention to the feelings expressed by the characters ▪ Pay attention to the characters' actions ▪ Highlight or take notes about the characters' feelings and learn if they change from the beginning to the end of the story

Fiction		
Genre	**Features of the Genre**	**Strategies**
Fantasy	■ A story that could never really happen ■ Some or all of the characters are made up ■ The setting may not be a real place. ■ Animals and imaginary characters may talk and communicate with realistic characters. ■ Time does not always pass in minutes, hours, and days	■ Pay special attention to the story elements: setting, characters, and time ■ Highlight or take notes on the important elements ■ Do not be surprised or fooled by something unexpected in reality
Science fiction	■ The main events might really happen, but something about them may not seem real	■ Look for the use of time travel or animals that talk ■ Look for imaginary settings
Fable	■ A short tale that usually teaches a moral or a lesson ■ Characters are often nonliving things or animals that talk and act like human beings	■ Look for animals that act like humans ■ Pay attention to the story elements ■ Focus on the conflict, the problem, and the solution ■ Look for the lesson learned by one or more of the characters

Realistic fiction	■ The characters are fictional (not real), but the story is based on situations that could really happen ■ The setting is often a place the reader knows or could recognize	■ Pay attention to the story elements ■ Highlight or take notes about the setting, characters, and events
Folktale	■ Plot is important ■ There is often a lesson to be learned ■ Folktales deal with ordinary people who do not have special powers ■ A <u>tall tale</u> is a folktale that exaggerates details to help the reader understand the meaning of the tale	■ Pay attention to the plot and the lesson learned ■ Highlight or take notes on important information ■ Highlight or take notes on the lesson taught and learned at the end of the tale ■ Highlight or take notes on the exaggerations the author uses to tell the tale

Poetry		
Genre	Features of the Genre	Strategies
Poetry	■ Not always written in full and complete sentences ■ The author's choice of words is important ■ A great deal of meaning is provided in each line ■ Figurative language is important in poems ■ Words are often used to create a sensory image for the reader ■ Some poems use rhyme	■ Read the poem more than one time 1. Look for the main idea or theme of the poem 2. Now focus your attention on the sensory imagery the writer is trying to present to the reader ■ Focus on your thoughts and feelings as you read the poem again ■ Highlight or take notes on the sensory images described by the author

CHART 2: WHAT GOOD READERS DO

Good readers think a lot when they read. This chart will help you understand the thinking that good readers use to help them understand the text they are reading.

Before you begin reading	▪ Think about the title ▪ Look at the graphic organizers included with the text ▪ What do you know about the topic that might help you understand what the author is saying in the text ▪ Has the author included bold print headings to help you organize and understand the information in the text
While you are reading	▪ Think about: ▪ the story elements ▪ the details in the text ▪ the text structure ▪ the order of events ▪ the characters' actions, and feelings and how they change from the beginning to the end of the story ▪ Think about the story structure. Is there: ▪ a problem and solution ▪ cause and effect ▪ a sequence of events ▪ Think about the main idea of the text: ▪ identify important details ▪ Question the text: ▪ do you understand what the author is saying ▪ do you understand the characters' feelings

- ■ Draw conclusions and make inferences:
  - ■ sometimes an author does not write everything the reader needs to know in the text. Instead, the author includes enough information, or clues, for the reader to draw a conclusion or make an inference about what is happening in the story
  - ■ the reader has to think along with the author and draw a logical conclusion about the author's intended meaning
- ■ Pay attention to the words the author uses:
  - ■ if the words are new to you, use context clues to help you understand the meaning
  - ■ does the author use words to help the reader create an image in the reader's mind
- ■ Monitor your thinking:
  - ■ if your mind stops thinking about the words you are reading, stop and read the section again
  - ■ if you find that you do not understand the text, go back and read it again

After you finish reading	■ Read the questions carefully ■ Understand the question before you select or construct your answer

CHART 3: UNDERSTANDING AND ANSWERING THE QUESTIONS

There are two ways to think about the questions on the ELA test.

The question can be a literal question or an inferential question. Understanding the two types of questions will help you select or write the best answer for the question.

LITERAL QUESTIONS

A literal question asks for a fact or information that comes directly from the story. The author tells you the answer to this question in the text. There are two ways to find the answers to a literal question.

1. The author uses the exact words that you will need to answer the question. You can find the words you need to answer the question in one sentence. You can look back in the text and find the words you need to select the best multiple-choice answer. You can also use the author's words to help you write a constructed response.

2. The author tells you the information in the text, but you will need to look in more than one sentence to find the answer. For this question, you have to think about how the ideas or information in the text are related to each other. The question might ask you about the order of events in a story. You can look in the story to find the correct events and then search in another sentence for the event that happens next.

Here are some phrases that you may see in a literal question
■ Who is the main character in the story? ■ Fill in the chart to show what happens next. ■ Which detail best completes the chart? ■ According to the article… ■ According to the poem… ■ According to the author… ■ What happened before… ■ What happened after… ■ Use details from the story in your answer. ■ Give examples from the text to show… ■ Which sentence belongs in the empty box? ■ What advice does the author give you…

When you see these words in the question, it is probably a literal question. If you do not remember the answer, go back and look for the answer in the words the author used in the text.

INFERENTIAL QUESTIONS

To answer an inferential question, the reader has to think about the ideas and information included in the text. The author has included the information the reader needs to understand the meaning of the story, but has not written the exact words that will be used to answer the question.

The reader may need to draw a conclusion about a character's feelings. The reader may need to draw a conclusion from the facts presented in the text. The reader may need to think about what he or she knows about the topic of the story and let this connection help him or her draw a logical conclusion or inference to answer an inferential question.

Here are some phrases that you may see in an inferential question

- What is the main idea of the passage?
- What is this story mostly about?
- What is this poem mostly about?
- What is this article mostly about?
- Which is the most important detail in the text?
- Which statement best describes...
- How did the character feel when...
- What is the author's point of view?
- The author mostly likely wrote this story to...
- Read this line from the text. This sentence (or word) most likely means...
- Which sentence from the story is an opinion?
- What would be another good title for this story?
- The person telling this story most likely...
- In this text the word _____ most likely means...
- How do you know the character felt _____? Use details from the story in your answer.

Remember—when you answer an inferential question, the answer is based on a conclusion you have made from using the information the author stated in the text.

Chapter 2

READING COMPREHENSION AND CONSTRUCTED-RESPONSE QUESTIONS

A constructed-response question is different from a multiple-choice question. A constructed-response question does not give you possible answers. You need to construct the answer.

Think about the word "construct." **Construct** means to build. When you build, you put parts together to create something. That is just what a reader does to answer a constructed-response question. The reader uses information from the story to prepare a written response.

CONSTRUCTING THE RESPONSE

The information for the answer comes from the story. The reader has to think about the meaning of the story. To answer the question the reader may need to

- complete a graphic organizer.
- draw a conclusion.
- make a prediction, or
- think about the characters' feelings.

You will find constructed-response questions on the reading and listening portions of the New York State ELA Test.

GUIDED PRACTICE AND TEST YOUR SKILLS

This chapter provides instruction and practice in answering constructed-response questions. The stories in this chapter are the same stories used in Chapter 1. The first three passages include guided practice that will explain the thinking process that readers use to answer a constructed-response question.

The last reading passage will Test Your Skills. The answers are not included in this chapter. You will find the answers in the answer key at the back of the book.

Remember to use the charts in Chapter 1 to help you remember the strategies that good readers use.

GUIDED PRACTICE 1

The first story is a personal narrative. Think about the characters' feelings as you read the story.

Remember…the characters' thoughts and feelings can help the reader know more about the story.

Swim to Win

When Kate was 14 she swam on a high school swim team. Kate's team, the Spartans, wanted to win the championship. Their rival team, the Sharks, also wanted to win the championship. With one meet left in the season, the Spartans and Sharks were in a tie for first place. The final swim meet was one week away. The Spartans  would swim against the Sharks! The winners of this meet would be the champions.

The Sharks' coach wanted his team to win. The Sharks practiced twice a day. They practiced in the morning and in the afternoon. The Spartans' coach wanted his team to win. The Spartans practiced twice a day. They practiced after school, took a break, and practiced again in the evening.

The day of the final swim meet was here. Both teams were ready. The crowd cheered as each girl swam as fast as she could. When the meet was over the Spartans went home very happy!

Directions:

Now look at three different constructed-response questions for this story. Follow the thinking used by good readers in answering the questions.

1. Give **two** examples from the story that show the Spartans wanted to win the swimming championship.

    1.

    2. _____

Did you notice…?

The question asks for two examples. There is one line for each example. Write one sentence for each example.

WHAT GOOD READERS DO AND THINK

Return to the story and read to find two examples that will answer the question. Use this information to construct the response.

The author said:

The Spartans practiced twice a day. They practiced after school, took a break, and practiced again in the evening.

Use the details from the story to construct the response.

Response to question 1:

Give **two** examples from the story that show the Spartans wanted to win the swimming championship.

1. The Spartans practiced after school.

2. The Spartans practiced again in the evening.

A constructed-response question can also look like a graphic organizer. Some of the information will be included. The reader must fill in the missing details to answer this type of constructed-response question.

2. The chart below shows what happens in the story. Complete the chart using details from the story.

WHAT HAPPENS IN THE STORY

The Spartans want to beat the Sharks and win the championship.

The Spartans are happy because they won the meet and are the champions.

Did you notice...?
   Look at the details included in the graphic organizer. The details are from the beginning and the end of the story.

WHAT GOOD READERS DO AND THINK

Think about the order of events.

There are two boxes to complete.

Look back in the story for two things that happened before the Spartans went home happy.

Use these details to complete the response.

Did you notice…?

This question is asking for the same information as question 1. The answer is constructed in a different form, and the correct order of events is important.

Response to question 2:

WHAT HAPPENS IN THE STORY

The Spartans want to beat the Sharks and win the championship.

The Spartans practiced after school.

The Spartans came back in the evening and practiced a second time.

The Spartans are happy because they won the meet and are the champions.

There may be a question like this on the ELA test. Use details from the story to construct the response.

3. How do you know that the Spartans won the championship? Use details from the story in your answer.

_____

_____

_____

_____

_____

WHAT GOOD READERS DO AND THINK

The author did not say the Spartans won.
The characters' actions and feelings help tell the story.
The Spartans went home very happy.
The team would be happy if they won the championship.

Use this information to construct the response.

Response to question 3:

How do you know that the Spartans won the championship? Use details from the story in your answer.

<u>The Spartans felt ready for the final meet. The girls were happy when they went home. I know the team would be happy if they won the meet.</u>

It is important to include details from the story in a constructed response. There is an appendix at the back of this book that will help you understand how a response is scored.

GUIDED PRACTICE 2

The next practice is a nonfiction article. The author describes the life cycle of a frog. Think about the sequence of events as you read the article.

A Frog's Life

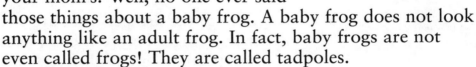

When you were born, your family and friends saw how much you looked like your mother or your father. Perhaps your eyes are the same shape as your dad's. Or maybe your chin looks just like your mom's. Well, no one ever said those things about a baby frog. A baby frog does not look anything like an adult frog. In fact, baby frogs are not even called frogs! They are called tadpoles.

Life Begins in an Egg

Frogs lay their eggs in water or wet places. The eggs are in a jellylike substance and clump together. This large clump of eggs is called frog spawn. Some frogs can lay more than 1,000 eggs. Only a few of the eggs will survive to grow into adult frogs.

Life for a frog begins when a single cell inside the egg begins to split. Each surviving egg is called an embryo. The life that is now growing in the egg looks like a tadpole. In three weeks the tadpole will hatch with gills, a mouth, and a tail.

The Tadpole Begins to Change

In five weeks the tadpole begins another cycle of change. First, it starts to grow legs. Next, the lungs begin to develop. The front legs will begin to grow before the tail disappears. The tadpole is now

called a froglet. It looks like a tiny frog with a tail! Just a few more weeks and the cycle will be complete. Sixteen weeks after hatching, the frog has gone through a complete growth cycle.

Now the baby looks like its mother and father.

Directions:

Now look at two constructed-response questions for this passage. Follow the thinking used by good readers in answering the questions.

4. According to the article, what are **two** ways that a baby frog changes before it completes the growth cycle and becomes an adult frog.

    1. _____

    2. _____

WHAT GOOD READERS DO AND THINK

The author describes many changes in the cycle. Find two details to include in the response.

Response to question 4:

According to the article, what are **two** ways that a baby frog changes before it completes the growth cycle and becomes an adult frog.

1. The baby frog will grow gills, a mouth, and a tail.

2. Lungs will begin to develop when it is a tadpole.

5. The article describes the changes in the life cycle of a frog. Use details from the article to complete the following web.

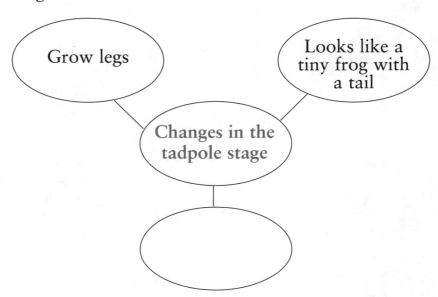

WHAT GOOD READERS DO AND THINK

Think about the question.
The changes must happen at the tadpole stage.
Use the **bold** headings to locate this stage in the article.
Find a third change that happens to a tadpole.
Write this detail in the empty circle.

Did you notice…?
The sequence of events is important in this question. The detail for this response can only be found in the section called The Tadpole Begins to Change.

Response to question 5:

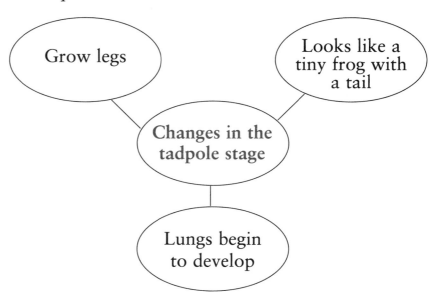

It is important to understand the question before writing the response. There are many details in this article. Be sure to look in the correct section of the article.

GUIDED PRACTICE 3

Readers will make connections to what they already know to help construct responses. But the response must match the details from the story.

Winter Vacation

"Wow, can you believe our winter vacation starts next week!"

"I know, Jim. You and your sister will have two weeks of winter fun," said Dad.

"I remember the fun you and Susan had last year," said Mom as she passed the carrots to Jim.

Susan started to laugh. "Hey, Dad. Do you remember when you and Mom tried to ride down the steep hill together on the toboggan?"

"I sure remember!" said Jim. "I laughed so hard I fell down."

"But not as hard as I did." said Dad. "It's a good thing I was wearing my snowsuit."

Mom was remembering Dad rolling down the hill next to her. She was laughing when she said, "Let's have a different kind of fun this vacation."

Directions:

Now look at two constructed-response questions for this passage. Follow the thinking used by good readers in answering the questions.

6. How do Jim and Susan feel about winter vacations? Use details from the story in your answer.

_____

_____

_____

_____

WHAT GOOD READERS DO AND THINK

The author is using the characters' dialogue to tell this story.

The characters' words can tell the reader how they feel.

Punctuation marks can help show emotion.

Did you notice…?

The exclamation mark in the first sentence shows that the speaker is excited about the winter vacation.

Dad said that they will have two weeks of winter fun.

Mom remembers the fun they all had last year.

The family is describing a vacation when they had a lot of fun and laughs together.

Use these details to draw a conclusion about how the children feel about winter vacations.

Response to question 6:

How do Jim and Susan feel about winter vacations? Use details from the story in your answer.

Jim and Susan are talking about the fun times they had on their last winter vacation. They remember laughing when Dad rolled down the hill. I think Jim and Susan really like winter vacations.

Include details from the story in the constructed response. Details show that you understood the meaning of the story.

7. In the story the father says:

"It's a good thing I was wearing my snowsuit."

What did he mean? Use details from the story in your answer.

_____

_____

_____

_____

WHAT GOOD READERS DO AND THINK

Jim just said he laughed so hard he fell.
Dad said, "But not as hard as I did."
That means that Dad fell, too.
Dad could have been hurt when he fell.
He laughed because he did not get hurt.
The snowsuit was thick, and that is why Dad did not get hurt when he fell.

Use the details to support the conclusion.

Response to question 7:

In the story the father says:

"It's a good thing I was wearing my snowsuit."

What did he mean? Use details from the story in your answer.

Dad fell when he was riding the toboggan with Mom. He might have been hurt if he had not been wearing a thick snowsuit. Dad was glad the snowsuit saved him from getting hurt.

TEST YOUR SKILLS

Directions:

Read the poem. Then answer the constructed-response questions.

Baby Sister

My sister learned to walk today,
   She took a step or two.
"That's great," I said, "Let's go out and play."
   Mom said, "Wait a day or two."

My sister walked and then she fell down,
   Her diapers softened the fall.
I guess Mom's right, she's up and she's down,
   Not ready to play at all.

My sister will need lots of practice,
   To be steady on her feet.
I'd really like to wait for you, Sis,
   But for now, I'll run with Pete!

1.   Read this line from the poem:

   Mom said, "Wait a day or two."

Use details from the poem to explain what the mother meant when she said these words.

_____

_____

_____

_____

_____

2. Read this line from the poem:

Her diapers softened the fall.

Use details from the poem to explain what the mother meant when she said these words.

_____

_____

_____

_____

_____

Answers are on page 154.

Congratulations! You have finished the practice for constructed-response questions.

The following chart will help you remember how to construct a complete response.

Completing charts	■ You will use details from the text to complete a chart. ■ Look back in the story for the words the author used. ■ Include the adjectives used by the author to describe an item in detail. ■ Write the details in the order they occurred in the text.
Constructing a response in one sentence	If one or two lines are provided, you may be able to answer the question in one sentence. When you construct the sentence: ■ write the name of the character you are writing about. **Do not use pronouns in your response.** ■ include details from the story in your answer.
Constructing a response in a paragraph	If more than two lines are provided for the answer, you will need to write a brief paragraph. When you construct the paragraph: ■ write the name of the character you are writing about. **Do not use pronouns in your response.** ■ write a topic sentence and use details from the story to support your topic sentence.

Write as neatly as you can. If your answer cannot be read, it cannot be scored.

Chapter 3

LISTENING COMPREHENSION

Day 2 of the ELA test begins with a listening comprehension test. This will measure how well you remember a story that is read to you.

LISTENING COMPREHENSION

Listening for information is something we do everyday. Talking with your family or friends is a listening activity.

Think about this: You are at school, and your friend tells you about a funny thing that happened to him. You listen as your friend tells the story. When you get home, you share the funny story with your family.

You think about the story your friend told you. You may not remember every word your friend said. But you do remember the main events and the important details. You remember the most important people in the story. You listened and remembered enough information to retell the story to your family. That is listening comprehension.

WHAT TO EXPECT ON THE TEST

You will listen to the story two times. Then you will answer 4 multiple-choice questions and 2 constructed-response questions. You will have 35 minutes to answer the questions.

Listen carefully each time the story is read to you. You can take notes the second time the story is read to you.

TAKING AND USING NOTES

Since this is a listening test, you will not have a copy of the story to read. This means that you cannot look back at the story to help you answer the questions. This is the reason you may want to take notes. You can look back at your notes to help you answer the questions.

Taking notes may be a new skill for you. This chapter will give you some tips for listening and taking notes. It will also give you guided practice on using notes to help you answer questions.

LISTENING TIPS

While the story is being read:

- Focus your attention on the reader.
- Make eye contact with the reader to help filter out other distracting noises.
- Think about what is being read.
- Try to form a picture of the story in your mind as you listen.

The first time you listen:

- You want to understand what the story is mostly about. Listen for the story elements.

- While you are listening, think about:
    - The title—does the title give you an idea of what the story might be about?
    - The main idea—what is happening in the story?
    - The main characters—who are the most important characters in the story?
    - The setting—is it important to remember where the story takes place?

- The main event—what happens in the beginning, the middle, and the end of the story?
- As you wait for the second reading to begin, write down a few words that will help you remember some of story elements.

Get ready to listen to the story again.

Now that you know the main idea of the story, you can focus your attention on the supporting details. You may want to take a few quick notes to help you remember these details. The notes should be short. Do not write sentences. Write names or places. Just write the words that will help you remember the important details.

Think about:

- The characters—did the characters say or do something that helps you understand their feelings?

- The setting—is it important to remember when and where the story takes place?

- The main event:
  - Was there a problem and a solution?
  - Was there a cause and an effect?

- The sequence of events—is it important to remember the order of the events in the story?

- The ending—how did the story end?
  - Was a problem solved?
  - Did the characters change in any way?
  - Did a character learn a lesson in this story?

Keep writing notes after the story is finished. Write all that you remember while the important details are still in your memory. Write them down before looking at the questions.

LISTENING AND TAKING NOTES

Listening and taking notes takes practice. There is a lot to think about. The listener has to focus on the story and think about what is important. The second time the story is read, the listener has to listen to the story and take notes at the same time.

FIND A PARTNER

The best way to practice listening is to listen. Ask some-one to read the practice stories to you. Then, read the guided practice together. The guided practice will help you learn how to take notes. The guide will show you how to use these notes to answer the questions that follow the story.

GUIDED PRACTICE AND TEST YOUR SKILLS

This chapter provides instruction and practice in listening to a story and answering multiple-choice and constructed-response questions. This will test your listening compre-hension.

The first two listening passages include guided practice. The guided practice will help your understand which information is important to include in your notes as you listen to the story the second time. The guided practice will also help you select the comprehension strategies to use in answering the questions you will be asked.

The last listening passage will Test Your Skills. No guid-ance is offered while you listen, take notes, and answer the questions. The answers are included in the answer key at the back of the book.

GUIDED PRACTICE 1

The directions below are similar to the directions for the listening section of the state ELA test.

Directions:

You will listen to a story called "A Special Birthday Celebration." Then you will answer some questions about the story.

You will listen to the story twice. The first time you hear the story, listen carefully but do not take notes. As you listen to the story the second time, you may want to take notes. You may use these notes to answer the questions that follow. Your notes will NOT count toward your final score.

A Special Birthday Celebration

The big day is almost here. Sam has been keeping his room clean and doing all his chores for the last six weeks. He even finished his homework every day before watching TV in the evening.

Sam is going to be nine years old on Saturday. He is having a special birthday celebration. The day will start with a special breakfast cooked by his grandmother. After breakfast, Sam will meet nine of his friends at The Pirate's Cove to play a round of miniature golf. Sam and his friends will finish the afternoon with a birthday lunch at their favorite pizza restaurant. Sam knows that he will have a great time with all of his friends, but he is waiting for the special surprise that his mom and dad have planned for the evening.

Sam has worked very hard for the last six weeks to show his parents that he can be responsible. His parents have said that they are very proud of him and that he has earned his special birthday celebration.

After dinner tonight, Sam is going shopping with his mom and dad. They are going to Puppy Palace. Sam will get the puppy he has always wanted. The puppy is the best celebration!

Think about the following questions before you listen for the second time. The words in bold print are possible answers.

1. What is the title? **A Special Birthday Celebration**
2. What is the main idea? **Sam is having a birthday. Sam wanted a dog for his birthday.**
3. Who is the main character? **Sam**
4. What is the setting? **Sam's house, the golf course, the pet store**
5. What is the main event? **Sam gets a puppy.**

Quick Notes

There may be time to write a few quick notes before the second reading begins. Some helpful notes could be:

> Celebration
> Sam
> Birthday with friends and friends
> Wants a puppy

Did you notice…?

The quick notes are just a few words. The words could help the listener remember this story. Listen for details as you hear the story the second time.

Now listen to the story for the second time.

Directions:

Use a separate piece of paper to take notes as you listen. Remember to finish writing the notes before looking at the questions.

Notes

The notes might look something like this:

> Celebration—birthday, Sam is 9, Saturday
> Sam wants a puppy
>   Cleans room, does homework, is ready for a pet
> Birthday party
>   Breakfast—grandma—morning
>   Golf and pizza with friends—afternoon
>   Shopping with parents—dinner
> Parents proud
> Sam can get puppy

Use your notes to help you answer the following questions:

1. Sam met his friends to
 A. have breakfast.
 B. go to the shopping mall.
 C. watch a movie.
 D. play golf and eat pizza.

WHAT GOOD LISTENERS DO AND THINK

This is a detail from the story. The answer is D. Look at the note-taking page to see how the short notes can help answer this question.

2. Read the sentences from the story.

> Sam will get the puppy he always wanted.
> The puppy is the best celebration.

These sentences show that
A. Sam was surprised.
B. Sam enjoyed his birthday.
C. Mom and Dad planned a surprise for Sam.
D. Sam has wanted a puppy for a very long time.

WHAT GOOD LISTENERS DO AND THINK

The correct answer is D. The author gave the information to answer this question. Think about the words always wanted. Sam is nine years old. Sam has wanted a puppy for a long time.

---

3. Give two examples from the story that show Sam was ready to take care of a puppy.

1. _____

2. _____

WHAT GOOD LISTENERS DO AND THINK

Sam did three things to show he could take care of a puppy. Use any two in the constructed response.

1. Sam cleaned his room.
2. Sam did all of his chores.
3. Sam finished his homework before watching TV.

Look at the short notes and see how they can help answer this question.

4. Sam did many things to show he was ready to take care of a puppy. This shows that Sam is
   A. happy.
   B. responsible.
   C. busy.
   D. upset.

WHAT GOOD LISTENERS DO AND THINK

The answer is B. This is a question about the character and is a vocabulary question. Think about the four choices. Think about the reason Sam did what he did. Sam wanted to show he could take care of a puppy. The best word for that is "responsible."

---

5. Sam's parents were proud of Sam and gave him a puppy for his birthday. Explain why Sam's parents felt proud. Use details from the story in your answer.

WHAT GOOD LISTENERS DO AND THINK

Think about the main idea of this story to answer this question. Sam wanted a puppy and had to prove he could take care of a puppy. Sam worked hard to clean his room, do his chores, and finish his homework. Include these details in the answer.

Possible answer:

Sam worked hard to keep his room clean and do his chores. He did this to show that he could take care of himself and take care of a puppy. His parents were proud because Sam worked hard and showed them that he was ready to have a puppy.

6. According to this story, which sentence is an opinion?
   A. Sam cleaned his room and finished his chores.
   B. Mom and Dad have a present for Sam.
   C. The puppy is the best celebration.
   D. Sam will be nine years old on Saturday.

WHAT GOOD LISTENERS DO AND THINK

The correct answer is C. An opinion is something that cannot be proved to be true. Another way of thinking about an opinion is to ask if it is something you can agree or disagree with. The word **best** helps you select this answer. Sam thinks the puppy is the best part of the celebration. This is Sam's opinion. Someone could disagree and think that the golf was the best part of the day.

GUIDED PRACTICE 2

Use the same thinking in this practice. Ask someone to read the next story to you. Follow the same directions as in Guided Practice 1. Have a piece of paper ready to take notes.

Roger Plans for a Snow Day

I don't usually watch the weather report, but tonight is different. Tomorrow could be the day. I had to find out for myself.

There was a buzz of excitement in the halls at school today. Everyone was hoping the big storm would come during the night. If the storm did come, we could get more than 36 inches of snow. That is more than 3 feet of snow. My kid sister is only 3 feet tall. The snow could be over her head.

I have never seen that much snow. I have lived in Florida most of my life. My family moved to the Adirondack Mountains last summer. This will be my first snowstorm.

The weather man just said there is a 95% chance the storm will hit our area. It will start late tonight and end by dinnertime tomorrow. We could really have a snow day.

I called my three best friends. I needed to know what to do if it snows all day. We made our plans right away. Jimmy decided that we should all spend the night at his house. This way, no one will have to walk or ask their parents to drive during the snowstorm in the morning. We would all bring our sleeping bags, a favorite inside game, and our outside winter clothes.

All I had to do now was convince my parents to let me stay at Jimmy's house tonight. I can hear their thoughts now. "But tomorrow is a school day. What if the weather report is incorrect?" I prepared my answers. Tomorrow could be a great day.

I got myself ready. I went downstairs with my sleeping bag, my favorite indoor game, my outside winter clothes, and my hopes that I could convince my parents to let me go to Jimmy's house. I did not expect the surprise waiting for me in the family room!

I was greeted by my three best friends. Each had a sleeping bag, their favorite indoor game, and their outside winter clothes. My parents had arranged for them all to spend the night at my house. My parents said they wanted me to enjoy my very first snow day playing in my new house with my new best friends.

Quick Notes

Write a few quick thoughts on a separate piece of paper before listening to the story again. As you listen to the story the second time, you may want to take more notes. You can use these notes to answer the questions that follow.

Now listen to the story for a second time.

Notes

The notes might look something like this:

Roger, Jimmy, and two friends
Roger's mom and dad
Moved to mountains
Weather report—may be snowstorm—more than
  3 feet
Maybe a snow day
Roger never saw snow—lived in Florida
Boys plan sleepover at Jimmy's
Bring 3 things with them
Roger surprised—friends at his house
Roger—parents say he should have first snow day at
  his new house with new friends

WHAT GOOD LISTENERS DO AND THINK

Note taking:

    Name of important characters
    Main events
    Important details to explain the events
    Important changes in the story
    The story ending
    Character's feelings

Did you notice...?
   The last line in the notes is almost a full sentence. This was the final important detail from the story. The complete thought could be written down before reading the first question.

Directions:

Use your notes to help you answer the following questions.

7. According to this story, this is Roger's first snow day because
   A. it is the first snowstorm of the season.
   B. this is his first winter in the Adirondack Mountains.
   C. this is the first year he is in school.
   D. it is the first day of winter.

WHAT GOOD LISTENERS DO AND THINK

The correct answer is **B**. This is a detail from the story.

Did you notice...?
   The notes just had the word "mountain." That could be a quick note that could help answer this question.

8. The weather report predicted
   A. more than 3 feet of snow.
   B. a cold and windy day.
   C. snow and freezing rain.
   D. there would be no school tomorrow.

WHAT GOOD LISTENERS DO AND THINK

The correct answer is A. This is a detail from the story. Look at the notes. This is an important detail to include. Use just a few words to help you remember.

---

9. Read the following line from the story.

   There was a buzz of excitement in the halls at school today.

   This sentence means:
   A. There were bees in the halls at school.
   B. The children were excited and talking about the predicted snowstorm.
   C. The students were running through the halls.
   D. Jimmy was planning a sleepover.

WHAT GOOD LISTENERS DO AND THINK

The correct answer is B. This is an example of figurative language. The author uses the word "buzz" to create an image of students with the high energy of bees buzzing near their hive. The reader has to connect the image to the meaning in this story.

10. Use details from the story to complete the following web.

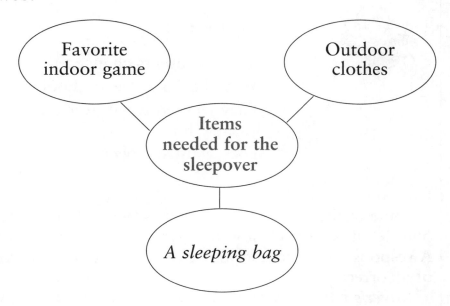

11. The boys did not spend the night at Jimmy's house. Explain why their plans were changed. Use details from the story in your answer.

_____

_____

_____

WHAT GOOD LISTENERS DO AND THINK

There are details that must be included in this response. The details include

Roger's parents changed the plans.
They did not expect school to be open tomorrow.
They wanted Roger to enjoy his first snow day in his new house.
They wanted Roger to be with his new friends.

Did you notice…?

Some of the details are the words the author used in the story. The second detail is a conclusion that was made using the details from the story. A response that includes those details would be correct. Here is a sample of a correct response:

Roger's parents thought there would be a snow day. They wanted Roger to enjoy his first snow day in his new house. They also wanted him to be with his new friends.

12. Another good title for this story would be:
   A. The Big Storm
   B. Roger's First Snow Day
   C. The Weather Report
   D. The Sleepover

WHAT GOOD LISTENERS DO AND THINK

The correct answer is B. Think about the main idea of the story. The story is mostly about Roger's first snow day. The storm, the weather report, and the sleepover were supporting details.

TEST YOUR SKILLS

Directions:

You will listen to a story called "A Slumber Party." Then you will answer some questions about the story. You will listen to the story twice. The first time you hear the story, listen carefully but do not take notes. As you listen to the story the second time, you may want to take notes. You may use these notes to answer the questions that follow. Your notes will NOT count toward your final score.

Notes

A Slumber Party

"Mom, where is Pinky? She is my favorite stuffed animal. I can't leave home without her."

"I know that, Sally," says Mom. "Pinky is sitting next to your sleeping bag."

I am going to my first slumber party tonight. I am excited and nervous at the same time. Jane and I have been best friends for six years. We met when we were in nursery school. We play together almost every day.

I stay at Jane's house for dinner all the time. We like to pretend we are sisters. But I have always gone home to sleep in my own room. Tonight will be different. I will be spending the whole night at Jane's house.

Mom is worried that I might get homesick in the middle of the night. I told her not to worry. I will take three special things with me so I will feel right at home in Jane's house.

That's why I need Pinky. Pinky is a stuffed rabbit. Pinky's ears are long and soft. They tickle my nose when I hug her. That always makes me laugh.

I will also take Rocky. Rocky is a small pillow that looks like a raccoon. Mom made it for me when I was a baby. It has been washed so many times that the colors have faded, but I still take it with me everywhere I go.

The third item I will take is my sleeping pillow. My sleeping pillow is stuffed with feathers. I can wrap my arms around this pillow and get really cozy and comfortable. It even smells like home.

So, with these three special things, Jane's house will feel just like home. We can't wait to start our slumber party. We have rented four movies and are planning an "all-nighter." We wonder if we will both be awake when the last movie is finished!

1. Another good title for this story would be:
   A. A Night at Sally's House
   B. My Friend Jane
   C. Sally's First Sleepover
   D. Pinky Got Lost

2. Sally's mother was worried because
   A. Sally has never spent the night away from home.
   B. Sally does not know Jane very well.
   C. Sally does not like to watch movies.
   D. Sally is only three years old.

3. Jane and Sally first met
   A. in kindergarten.
   B. at a playground.
   C. at the movies.
   D. in nursery school.

4. Use details from the story to complete the chart.

Three important things Sally will take to the slumber party
A stuffed rabbit named Pinky
?
?

5. Explain why Sally will take three special things to Jane's house. Use details from the story in your answer.

_____

_____

_____

_____

_____

6. Read this line from the story:

   Mom is worried that I might get homesick in the middle of the night.

   If Sally gets homesick, she most likely
   A. will get sick because she stayed up all night.
   B. will wake up and feel sick.
   C. will miss her family because she is away from home.
   D. will get sick because she is not in her own bed.

Answers are on pages 155–156.

Congratulations! You have finished the practice for the listening portion of the ELA test.

 The following chart can help you remember how to take notes while you listen to a story.

The first time the story is read	Listen for ■ the main idea ■ the main characters ■ the setting ■ the problem and solution ■ the order of events ■ the ending
Before the story is read the second time	You will have a few brief moments. Write a list of the most important details that you remember.
The second time the story is read	You know what the story is about. Write a few words that will help you remember the most important information in the story. Your notes may look like a list. Remember—you will not have time to write complete sentences as you listen.

WRITING ASSESSMENT: THE EDITING PASSAGE

The New York State Grade 3 ELA Test assesses writing with a test in editing skills. This chapter will provide guided practice for the Grade 3 ELA writing test.

The writing test is the second section for day 2. To complete the writing test you will read a short paragraph and correct the mistakes that have been included. There will be errors in capital letters and punctuation only. There will not be any errors in spelling.

This chapter includes three paragraphs with guided practice and one paragraph to Test Your Skills. You will find the answers for the Test Your Skills paragraph in the answer key at the back of this book.

WHAT TO LOOK FOR WHEN YOU EDIT A PARAGRAPH

1. When looking for mistakes in capital letters:
   a. Does every sentence start with a capital letter?
   b. Does every proper name begin with a capital letter?
   c. Is there a capital letter in a noun that is not a proper noun?
   d. Does the word I appear correctly in the paragraph?

2. When looking for mistakes in punctuation:
   a. Does every sentence end with a punctuation mark?
   b. Is the punctuation mark you see the correct mark?

FINDING AND MARKING THE CORRECTIONS

The test paragraph will be very short. Read the entire paragraph to understand its meaning. Now, go back and read the paragraph a second time. As you read, look for mistakes in capitalization and punctuation.

When you find a mistake:

1. Draw a line through the mistake.
2. Write the correction above the error.

Here is an example of a mistake in capitalization.

Kate went to a movie with janet.

The sentence has a proper name that does not begin with a capital letter.

Here is the way to mark the mistake *and* make the correction.

Kate went to a movie with janet.

Janet (written above the crossed-out *janet*)

Did you notice…?

1. The mistake is marked by drawing a line through the word with the mistake.
2. The correction is written above the word that has the mistake.

It would also be correct to:

1. Cross out only the lowercase letter that is incorrect (j).
2. Write the correct capital letter (J) above the incorrect lowercase letter.

Here is an example of a mistake in punctuation.

Is John going to the movie with Kate.

Notice the mistake in the punctuation. This is a question, not a statement. The end punctuation is not correct. This is how you would mark and correct the mistake.

Kate?

Is John going to the movie with ~~Kate.~~

Did you notice...?

1. The mistake is the **period** at the end instead of a **question mark**.

2. The mistake is marked by drawing a line through the last word *and* the incorrect **punctuation**.

3. The correction is made by writing the last word *and* the correct **punctuation mark**.

SCORING THE WRITING TEST

The writing test is scored with a rubric. It is scored in a way that is quite different from scoring the reading and listening tests. A perfect score is 4. A point is earned for each mistake that is marked and corrected. However, points are taken away from the final score if a change is made that creates a new mistake.

There is a chart at the back of the book that explains the writing scoring rubric.

GUIDED PRACTICE

The guided practices will begin with directions that are like the directions on the state ELA test.

GUIDED PRACTICE 1

Directions:

Here is a paragraph a student wrote about his favorite game. The paragraph has some mistakes in capital letters and punctuation. Some sentences may have no mistakes. There are <u>no</u> mistakes in spelling. Read the paragraph and find the mistakes. Draw a line through each mistake in the paragraph. Then write the correction above it.

My favorite game is baseball. I like to watch it on TV.

i like to play it with my friends. I am on a team with

my friends Jim and pete. The team practices saturday

mornings at 10:00. I am the pitcher?

Correct the mistakes and check your answers with the answers provided. The corrections are in bold print. The mistakes are explained to you.

My favorite game is baseball. I like to watch it on TV.
I
~~i~~ like to play it with my friends. I am on a team with
                                  Pete   **Saturday**
my friends Jim and ~~pete~~. The team practices ~~saturday~~
                                                    pitcher.
mornings at 10:00. I am the ~~pitcher?~~

1. The word I is always written with a capital letter.
2. Pete is a proper name and must begin with a capital letter.
3. Saturday is a proper name and must begin with a capital letter.

4. The last sentence is <u>not</u> a question. The correct punctuation is a period. (*It would be correct to cross out the question mark and write a period above it.*)

Did you notice...?

It is easy to see the corrections that are made when the mistakes are crossed out and the corrections written above the word. The answer *would* be scored correct if only the capital letter or the punctuation was written above the error.

GUIDED PRACTICE 2

Directions:

Here is a paragraph a student wrote about learning to make cookies. The paragraph has some mistakes in capital letters and punctuation. Some sentences may have no mistakes. There are <u>no</u> mistakes in spelling. Read the paragraph and find the mistakes. Draw a line through each mistake in the paragraph. Then write the correction above it.

I am learning how to make chocolate chip cookies.

My mother is teaching me. she said that the cookies

will taste best if i put in milk chocolate chips. I mixed

the flour, sugar, butter, and eggs together. The cookies

have to bake for 15 minutes. When they are ready I

will share them with my Friends. Do you like choco-

late chip cookies.

Correct the mistakes and check your answers with the answers in the answer box. The corrections are in bold print. The mistakes are explained to you.

I am learning how to make chocolate chip cookies.

My mother is teaching me. ~~she~~ **She** said that the cookies

will taste best if ~~i~~ **I** put in milk chocolate chips. I mixed

the flour, sugar, butter, and eggs together. The cookies

have to bake for 15 minutes. When they are ready I

will share them with my ~~Friends~~ **friends**. Do you like choco-

late chip ~~cookies.~~ **cookies?**

---

1. She is the first word in the sentence and must be a capital letter.
2. The word I is always a capital letter.
3. The word friends is not a proper noun. It should <u>not</u> start with a capital letter.
4. The last sentence is a question. The correct punctuation is a question mark.

Did you notice...?
Read the sentence:

she said that the cookies will taste best if i put in milk chocolate chips.

There are two mistakes in this sentence. Both are mistakes in capital letters. This sentence *does not* need quotation marks. The narrator is *telling* the reader what the mother said. The mother is *not* speaking in this story. Adding quotation marks would create a new mistake. Points would be subtracted from the total writing score.

GUIDED PRACTICE 3

Directions:

Here is a paragraph a student wrote about a school field trip. The paragraph has some mistakes in capital letters and punctuation. Some sentences may have no mistakes. There are <u>no</u> mistakes in spelling. Read the paragraph and find the mistakes. Draw a line through each mistake in the paragraph. Then write the correction above it.

Miss Singer's class went on a field trip to the bronx Zoo. The children enjoyed the monkey exhibit the best? When the monkeys made silly noises, Miss Singer made silly noises. When the monkeys jumped up and down, Miss Singer also jumped up and down. everyone laughed when the monkeys climbed to the top of the cage and swung from their tails. miss Singer could not do that.

Correct the mistakes and check your answers with the answers provided. The corrections are in bold print. The mistakes are explained to you.

> Bronx
> Miss Singer's class went on a field trip to the ~~bronx~~
>
> Zoo. The children enjoyed the monkey exhibit the
> best.
> ~~best?~~ When the monkeys made silly noises, Miss
>
> Singer made silly noises. When the monkeys jumped
>
> up and down, Miss Singer also jumped up and down.
> Everyone
> ~~everyone~~ laughed when the monkeys climbed to the
>
> Miss
> top of the cage and swung from their tails. ~~miss~~ Singer
>
> could not do that.

1. The name of the zoo is the **Bronx Zoo.** The name of the zoo is a proper name. Both words in a proper name must begin with a **capital letter.**

2. The second sentence is <u>not</u> a question. The correct **punctuation** is a period.

3. The first word in a sentence always starts with a **capital letter. Everyone** must begin with a **capital letter.**

4. Miss also must begin with **a capital letter.**

Did you notice...?

The last sentence could have an exclamation mark as the end punctuation. However, the sentence is correct with a period. If an exclamation mark were added, it would not be incorrect. No points would be subtracted from the score if an exclamation point were added.

It is important to remember that the New York State Grade 3 writing test is an editing test and is *not* a test for revision. Do not change the language of the sentences. Simply look for errors in punctuation and capitalization. Cross out the mistake and write the correction above it.

TEST YOUR SKILLS

Directions:

Here is a paragraph a student wrote about a sunny day. The paragraph has some mistakes in capital letters and punctuation. Some sentences may have no mistakes. There are <u>no</u> mistakes in spelling. Read the paragraph and find the mistakes. Draw a line through each mistake in the paragraph. Then write the correction above it.

It is a warm and sunny day today? I think i will do my homework outside. My homework is to read a book about Michael jordan. I will bring out my new Rocking chair. The sun will feel wonderful.

Answers are on page 156.

Congratulations! You have finished the practice for the writing portion of the ELA test.

 This chart will help you remember the rules for punctuation.

Capital letters	■ The first word of a sentence begins with a capital letter. ■ Proper nouns begin with a capital letter. ■ The word "I" is always a capital letter.
Punctuation	■ All sentences end with a punctuation mark. ■ Sentences can end with a period, a question mark, or an exclamation point.

PRACTICE TEST 1

SESSION 1, DAY 1: READING COMPREHENSION

3 or 4 reading passages
20 multiple-choice questions
1 short constructed-response question
You will have 40 minutes to complete Session 1.

SESSION 2, DAY 2: LISTENING AND WRITING

1 listening selection
4 multiple-choice questions
2 short constructed-response questions
1 editing paragraph
You will have 35 minutes to complete Session 2.

TIMED TEST

Session 1: Book 1 is a timed test. For this session, you will be told how much time you have to complete each reading passage. The teacher will tell you when to begin reading each passage and answer the questions that follow. You will also be told when to stop. You should not have to rush. The instructions are designed to help you move through each reading passage in Book 1.

Session 2: Book 2 is completed on the second day. The listening test is first. You will listen to a story and answer questions about the story. You will listen to the story two times. Then, you will have 15 minutes to answer the questions.

The last section is the writing test. You will be given directions and complete a guided practice before you look at the test paragraph.

ANSWER SHEET

You will record the answers for the multiple-choice questions on a bubble sheet. You will answer the constructed-response questions in the test booklet. You will also write the corrections for the editing paragraph in the test booklet.

Use a pencil and fill in the circle with the letter that matches your answer. Be sure to fill in the circle completely. If you make a mistake, be sure to erase it completely.

Do not make any extra marks on your answer sheets. The answer sheets are scanned by a computer, and extra marks may be read as incorrect answers.

PRACTICE TEST 1

Remove the answer sheet from this book and begin. You will find the answers and explanations in an answer key at the back of the book.

SESSION 1, DAY 1

BOOK 1: READING

In this part of the test, you are going to do some reading. Then you will answer questions about what you have read.

Directions:

Read the story and answer questions 1–4. For each question, mark your answer on the answer sheet.

Sight to See

By Emily Singer

Cameron is visiting New York City with her father for the first time. He promised to take her to the top of the Empire State Building. He told her the view was something to see.

Cameron was excited as she rode the elevator to the top of the building. She was extremely excited to see the view from up there. She looked down and was surprised at how everything looked. "Everything looks so small from up here! The people look like little dolls. The cars look like toys," she yelled.

Go On

Her father nodded and said, "There is only one way to see things look smaller and that is to fly in a plane, helicopter, or spaceship."

"Yes," Cameron agreed, "but then things look too small. You can barely see the ground when you fly. From here, I can see the people on the ground and they all look like toys."

"That is very true. Can you imagine being able to look down and see the people on the ground when you are in a plane?" her father asked.

"The people would look smaller than ants. You would need to be a super hero to see them!" Cameron shouted.

After looking for a while, Cameron went back down to the street with her father. When she looked up, she said, "Dad, I bet I look as small as a toy to someone else now that I'm down here. Don't you think it is funny how that works?"

"Yes," her father agreed, "It is all about where you happen to be standing."

1. Read this line from the story.

   He told her the view was something to see.

   The sentence tells you that
   A. Cameron would have a view from the building.
   B. Cameron's father thought the view was very special.
   C. Cameron should look at the view.
   D. Cameron's father had never seen the view before.

2. Cameron was surprised to see the sights from the top of the building. This is **most likely**
   A. a view she sees every day.
   B. a view she did not enjoy.
   C. her first trip to the top of the Empire State Building.
   D. her first trip with her father.

3. According to this story, the people on the ground
   A. looked like little dolls.
   B. were too small to see.
   C. walked very fast.
   D. looked up to see her.

4. The author most likely wrote "Sights to See" to
   A. explain that people can look small.
   B. help the reader like New York.
   C. tell the reader that buildings can be tall.
   D. tell the reader about a personal story.

Directions:

Read this article. Then answer questions 5–9.

Seasons Change
By Sarah Reeves

All around the world seasons change, and the weather changes, too. Snow, rain, and lower temperatures tell you that winter is here. Summer, on the other hand, is a season with warm temperatures, sunny days, and night skies that never want  to become dark. Why does the sun stay up longer and the moon come up later in the summer? Learning about the summer solstice may help you to understand.

Go On

There is one day each year when the sun stays up longer than any other day. This day is called the summer solstice. It is the longest day of the year and the first day of summer. In the Northern Hemisphere, the summer solstice takes place around June 21, when the position of the sun is as far north as it ever gets during the year. Because the sun is closer to the Northern Hemisphere at the summer solstice, it is able to give more daylight for a longer time. This means longer days and shorter nights. The summer solstice happens only one day each year, but I have to say it is the brightest!

5. According to this article, signs of winter are
   A. children building a snowman.
   B. schools are closed.
   C. snow, rain, and low temperatures.
   D. ice and freezing rain.

6. According to this article, you can expect warm temperatures and sunny days
   A. in the summer.
   B. in the south.
   C. all around the world.
   D. only in the Northern Hemisphere.

7. The author of this article describes summer nights by saying

   night skies that never want to become dark.

   The author **most likely** wanted the reader to understand that
   A. the sun sets later at night in the summer.
   B. you cannot see the sunset in the summer.
   C. the stars are very bright in the summer.
   D. it is very dark in the summer.

8. According to this article, the summer solstice
    A. is a cold and rainy day.
    B. happens only in the Northern Hemisphere.
    C. Is the longest day of the year.
    D. occurs on July 21.

9. The author most likely wrote this article to
    A. share a funny story.
    B. give readers information about the summer solstice.
    C. describe a summer day.
    D. tell the reader that it is bright in the summer.

Directions:

Read the poem about attic treasure. Then answer questions 10–15.

Lost Attic Treasures
By Molly Stewart

> Attic: a room directly below the roof of a house.

I see an attic doorway
And guess at what's behind.
I want to turn the doorknob
I wonder what I'll find.

Maybe the key to the city
That's been lost for 20 years.
A suit of armor, a king's golden crown
A map to a treasure that's near.

Go On

Perhaps I may find a chest
Filled with ancient treasures.
And jewels worth a million
To buy a lifetime's pleasure.

But I guess I'll never know
Because when my imagination stopped.
I tried to turn the doorknob
And found the door was locked.

10. According to this poem, the lost treasure could be
   A. a box underneath a bed.
   B. a treasure buried in the sand.
   C. a million dollars.
   D. a surprise behind a locked door.

11. The chart below shows events from the story.

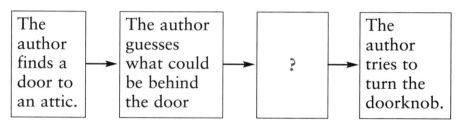

Which sentence belongs in the empty box?
   A. The attic holds a treasure.
   B. The author's imagination stops.
   C. The author discovers the door is locked.
   D. The author wakes up from a dream.

12. According to the poem, what are two things that the author imagined could be a lost attic treasure? Use details from the story in your answer.

1. There could be a million dollars

2. There could be a chest with ancient treasures

13. According to this poem, if the treasure was "jewels worth a million," the author would
   A. buy a car.
   B. buy a lifetime's pleasure.
   C. wear the jewels.
   D. be disappointed.

14. What is this poem mostly about?
   A. an empty attic room
   B. a treasure chest
   C. a locked door.
   D. the author's imagination.

15. The author of this poem can best be described as
   A. imaginative.
   B. serious.
   C. silly.
   D. forgetful.

Go On

Directions:

Read the story about learning how to play the cello.
Then answer questions 16–21.

Learning to Play the Cello
By Jonathan Wild

Have you ever wanted to play an instrument? Do you want something to do that you can enjoy your whole life? Do you want to do something that is both fun and challenging? Then the cello (pronounced *chello*) is the instrument for you! You can play in an orchestra and play a variety of musical pieces.

The cello is a stringed instrument. In order to play the cello you must know several important things.

First, there are many different kinds of cellos. Cellos come in three sizes. They are half, three-quarter, and full-size. The size you play depends on your size. Cellos come in different types of wood. Some are very expensive and can cost thousands of dollars.

Second, the cello has many different parts. The *endpin* is the long rod at the bottom of the cello. The strings run along a wooden piece called a *bridge*. The *fingerboard* is the black piece under the strings.

Third, the cello has four strings. They are the notes A, D, G, and C. You play the cello by running the *bow* back and forth across the strings near the bridge.

If you take cello lessons, you will learn a variety of ways to make different sounds. When you put the sounds together, you will have a musical piece. So, if you want to learn to play the cello, try your best and practice everyday. Your hard work will bring yourself and others much joy.

16. Read the chart below.

Parts of the Cello
Endpin
?
Fingerboard

Which word best completes the chart?
A. rosin
B. rod
C. bridge
D. notes

17. What is the most important detail when you select the proper cello?
A. your size
B. your favorite color
C. the wood
D. your favorite song

18. Read this line from the story.

> You can play in an orchestra and play a variety of musical pieces.

In this sentence the term "variety of musical pieces" most likely means
A. it is hard to play the cello.
B. you will learn to play many different songs.
C. you will learn only one song.
D. all the songs will sound the same.

Go On

19. Which sentence from the story is an opinion?
    A. The cello has four strings.
    B. You will bring yourself and others much joy.
    C. The endpin is a long rod.
    D. A cello can be very expensive.

20. Which statement best describes the author.
    A. The author can sing.
    B. The author plays in an orchestra.
    C. The author plays a variety of music.
    D. The author enjoys cello music.

21. What advice does the author give a reader who wants to learn to play the cello.
    A. Try your best and practice every day.
    B. Learn a variety of songs.
    C. Play the notes A, D, G, and C.
    D. Cellos come in different sizes.

SESSION 2, DAY 2

BOOK 2: LISTENING AND WRITING

PART 1: LISTENING

Directions:

In this part of the test, you are going to listen to a story called "The Mermaids." Then you will answer some questions about the story. You will have 15 minutes to answer the questions after you have listened to the story two times. You will listen to the story twice. The first time you hear the story, listen carefully but do not take notes. As you listen to the story the second time, you may want to take notes. You may use these notes to answer the questions that follow. Your notes will NOT count toward your final score.

Notes

The Mermaids
By Sara Meehl

There once was a girl named Maggie who lived near the ocean. Every day, she would go outside, sit on the beach, and watch the waves roll in and out. One day, something in the waves caught her eye.

She heard laughter, splashing, and talking coming from the ocean. It sounded very near. Maggie looked around to be sure it wasn't her sister playing a trick on her. But her sister was not there.

She looked at the waves again and saw a fin splash out of the water. It looked too big to belong to one of the fish that swam in the shallow water near the beach. Then, suddenly, two heads came into view.

"Hello," said one of the creatures. "I am Olivia, and this is Loretta. What is your name?"

"W-What" said Maggie, confused. "W-who are you? W-what are you doing in the water?"

"We are mermaids, of course!" said Loretta cheerfully.

"Really? I have never seen one before. Why are you at my house?" Maggie was very excited. Was she really talking to mermaids?

"My sister and I were just taking a swim and we saw you on the beach. We have never met a real girl before. You looked friendly so we thought we would say hello," said Olivia.

"Would you like to swim with us for a while?" asked Loretta.

"Yes, I would love that," said Maggie.

Maggie swam with her new mermaid friends until they heard a roaring sound coming from beneath the waves.

"That is our school bell," said Olivia. "We must go to school now. We will come back tomorrow if you would like to swim again."

"Yes. That would be great!" said Maggie. "See you tomorrow." Maggie could not wait to get home and tell her sister about her two new friends.

Maggie's sister did not believe her story. "There are no mermaids," she told Maggie. "You fell asleep in the hot sun and had a dream."

Maggie was upset. "That is not true. Come with me tomorrow and I will introduce you to my new friends."

The next day Maggie and her sister went to the beach and waited for Olivia and Loretta. Maggie's sister brought a camera and had it hanging from a strap on her neck. She did not believe Maggie. But, if the story was true, she was going to take a picture to show everyone that mermaids really do exist.

Maggie and her sister waited until it was almost dark. Their parents insisted that they come in for dinner. Maggie was disappointed that her friends had not come. Maggie's sister just laughed and said, "Sweet dreams," as she walked past Maggie and went inside for dinner.

As Maggie started to walk away she heard a voice that sounded like Olivia. It was Olivia!

"Where were you? I brought my sister here to meet you. Now she does not believe that you are real," said Maggie.

"We know. We saw her. We saw that she had a camera," said Loretta.

"That is why we could not come back to see you. The king of our land has warned us never to let humans see that we exist. Our king believes our lives would be different if people knew we really existed," said Olivia.

"We took a chance when we said hello to you. But we trust that you will keep us a secret," said Loretta.

"I understand," said Maggie. "Can we still be friends? I promise I will not tell anyone about you."

"Yes," said Olivia and Loretta at the same time. "Come back tomorrow and we will swim together again."

Go On

22. What caused the splashing that Maggie heard in the beginning of this story?
    A. small fish
    B. dolphins
    C. mermaids
    D. her sister

23. Read this sentence from the story.

    One day, **something besides the waves caught her eye.**
    The phrase "caught her eye" **most likely** means
    A. sand got in her eye.
    B. someone touched her face.
    C. the mermaids waved hello.
    D. she turned to look at something.

24. When Maggie saw the mermaids, she was **most likely** confused because
    A. she did not know where she was.
    B. she had never seen a mermaid before.
    C. she thought she was alone.
    D. she saw her sister.

25. Why did Olivia and Loretta stay away from Maggie when she brought her sister to meet them. Use details from the story in your answer.

    _____

    _____

    _____

    _____

26. The chart below shows what happened in the story. Complete the chart using details from the story.

WHAT HAPPENS IN THE STORY

Maggie meets two mermaids at the beach.

Maggie promises not to tell anyone that the mermaids are real.

27. This story can **best** be described as a

    A. fantasy.

    B. personal narrative.

    C. poem.

    D. news article.

Go On

PART 2: WRITING

Directions:

Look at the paragraph. There are some mistakes in this paragraph in capital letters and punctuation. Let's correct the mistakes together.

Draw a line through each part that has a mistake, and if a correction needs to be written, write it above the mistake.

Today is the first day of School. Twenty students are waiting to meet their new teacher. Mr. bedell is the best teacher in third grade? Mr. Bedell uses computer games to help his students study for tests. that makes studying fun!

Now take a look at the corrections you should have made.

Today is the first day of ~~School~~. Twenty students are *school*

waiting to meet their new teacher. Mr. ~~bedell~~ is the *Bedell*

best teacher in third ~~grade?~~ Mr. Bedell uses computer *grade.*

games to help his students study for tests. ~~that~~ makes *That*

studying fun!

Explanation:

Line 1 has one error. The word "school" is not a proper name. It should not have a capital letter.

Line 2 has one error. "Mr. Bedell" is a proper name; both words must begin with a capital letter.

Line 3 has one error. The sentence is a statement and not a question. The question mark must be changed to a period.

Line 4 has one error. The first word in a sentence must begin with a capital letter.

Note: The last line ends with a punctuation mark. The author placed it there to show emotion. If you changed the exclamation point to a period, it would not count as a mistake.

Go On

28. Here is a paragraph a student wrote about summer. The paragraph has some mistakes in capital letters and punctuation. Some sentences may have no mistakes. There are <u>no</u> mistakes in spelling.

Read the paragraph and find the mistakes.
Draw a line through each mistake in the paragraph.
Then write the correction above it.

Summer is my favorite time of year. i can swim in my

backyard pool. I plan a sleepover party every friday

night. My friends come over and we swim until it gets

dark. we end the night with a pizza party. Do you like

summer and sleepover parties.

PRACTICE TEST 2

SESSION 1, DAY 1: READING COMPREHENSION

3 or 4 reading passages
20 multiple-choice questions
1 short constructed-response question
You will have 40 minutes to complete Session 1.

SESSION 2, DAY 2: LISTENING AND WRITING

1 listening selection
4 multiple-choice questions
2 short constructed-response questions
1 editing paragraph
You will have 35 minutes to complete Session 2.

TIMED TEST

Session 1: Book 1 is a timed test. For this session, you will be told how much time you have to complete each reading passage. The teacher will tell you when to begin reading each passage and answer the questions that follow. You will also be told when to stop. You should not have to rush. The instructions are designed to help you move through each reading passage in Book 1.

Session 2: Book 2 is completed on the second day. The listening test is first. You will listen to a story and answer questions about the story. You will listen to the story two times. Then, you will have 15 minutes to answer the questions.

The last section is the writing test. You will be given directions and complete a guided practice before you look at the test paragraph.

ANSWER SHEET

You will record the answers for the multiple-choice questions on a bubble sheet. You will answer the constructed-response questions in the test booklet. You will also write the corrections for the editing paragraph in the test booklet.

Use a pencil and fill in the circle with the letter that matches your answer. Be sure to fill in the circle completely. If you make a mistake, be sure to erase it completely.

Do not make any extra marks on your answer sheets. The answer sheets are scanned by a computer, and extra marks may be read as incorrect answers.

ANSWER SHEET: PRACTICE TEST 2

BOOK 1

1. Ⓐ Ⓑ Ⓒ Ⓓ

2. Ⓐ Ⓑ Ⓒ Ⓓ

3. Ⓐ Ⓑ Ⓒ Ⓓ

4. Ⓐ Ⓑ Ⓒ Ⓓ

5. Ⓐ Ⓑ Ⓒ Ⓓ

6. Ⓐ Ⓑ Ⓒ Ⓓ

7. Ⓐ Ⓑ Ⓒ Ⓓ

8. Ⓐ Ⓑ Ⓒ Ⓓ

9. Ⓐ Ⓑ Ⓒ Ⓓ

10. Ⓐ Ⓑ Ⓒ Ⓓ

11. Ⓐ Ⓑ Ⓒ Ⓓ

12. Ⓐ Ⓑ Ⓒ Ⓓ

13. Ⓐ Ⓑ Ⓒ Ⓓ

14. Ⓐ Ⓑ Ⓒ Ⓓ

15. Ⓐ Ⓑ Ⓒ Ⓓ

16. Ⓐ Ⓑ Ⓒ Ⓓ

17. Ⓐ Ⓑ Ⓒ Ⓓ

18. Ⓐ Ⓑ Ⓒ Ⓓ

19. Read question 19 in your test book. Write your answer in the test book.

20. Ⓐ Ⓑ Ⓒ Ⓓ

21. Ⓐ Ⓑ Ⓒ Ⓓ

BOOK 2

22. Ⓐ Ⓑ Ⓒ Ⓓ

23. Ⓐ Ⓑ Ⓒ Ⓓ

24. Ⓐ Ⓑ Ⓒ Ⓓ

25. Read question 25 in your test book. Write your answer in the test book.

26. Read question 26 in your test book. Write your answer in the test book.

27. Ⓐ Ⓑ Ⓒ Ⓓ

PRACTICE TEST 2

Remove the answer sheet from this book and begin. You will find the answers and explanations in the answer key at the back of the book.

SESSION 1, DAY 1
BOOK 1: READING

In this part of the test, you are going to do some reading. Then you will answer questions about what you have read.

Directions:

Read the story and answer questions 1–5. For each question, mark your answer on the answer sheet.

Computers
By Carter Silvernell

Computers are normal to see in every day life. You may even have a computer in your room or house. Have you ever wondered how these amazing contraptions work? Have you wondered what computers might do in the future? Maybe you have wondered about the computers of the past. If you have wondered about computers, then you are going to enjoy this article.

Go On

The screen is an important part of the computer. Think about a game you might play on a computer. The picture you see on the screen is created by pixels. Pixels are tiny light bulbs that light up to a color. The pixels are arranged to make the image that you see. This arrangement is stored on the hard drive. When you play a game, the hard drive sends the pixels that are needed to create the picture you see on the screen.

In the future computers will be used in many different ways. Computers of the future will replace pencils, be put into our glasses to help us see, and even save lives. Computers will tell us if we are sick or healthy. This will be bad news if you want to fake being sick so you can stay home from school! Computers will also control small robots, called nanobots. Someday these computers may rove inside the body looking for a disease. They may help cure everything from the common cold to cancer.

In the 1980s, all of this was thought unlikely. Twenty-five years ago, kids like us would not really want a computer. The pictures on the screens were black and white. Video games were not made for computers until the early 1990s. Computer experts kept on trying. Without early dreams, we would not have Xbox 360s and Play Station 3. We would not have Halo 3 or any other popular games.

Computers have been amazing humans since their creation. The next time you use a computer consider its history. And don't forget—what is popular now will be old by tomorrow, but without the old stuff the new stuff would have never come to be.

1. According to this article, the picture on a computer screen is created by
   A. pixels.
   B. light.
   C. cameras.
   D. memory.

2. Read the chart below.

Computers of the Future
Will replace pencils
?
Will help save lives

Which phrase best completes the chart?
A. Will have more pixels
B. Will think for us
C. Will help us see
D. Will be replaced by robots

3. Read this line from the article.

Computers will also control small robots, called nanobots.

The word "nanobot" most likely means
A. very large.
B. new.
C. smart.
D. microscopic.

4. The author most likely wrote this article to
A. get the reader to like computers.
B. tell the reader computers are new.
C. teach the reader that computers have changed.
D. convince the reader to buy a computer.

Go On

5. According to this article, which statement is an opinion?
A. Computer experts kept on trying.
B. Kids like us would not really want a computer.
C. Pixels are tiny light bulbs that light up to a color.
D. In the future, computers will be used in many different ways.

Directions:

Read the poem "Autumn" and answer questions 6–10.

Autumn
By Dan Zuhlke

Some people call it Autumn.
Other people call it Fall.
The thing is whatever you call it
It's my favorite season of all.

Autumn's cool breeze
Is perfect for playing ball.
That is one reason why Autumn
Is my favorite season of all.

The leaves are colorful.
They always make me smile.
The only problem is
That they only stay for a while.

So during this time of year
I go outside because I know
After this wonderful season
Is the cold, winter snow.

I don't hate the snow.
I don't hate it at all.
Except it will be one more year
Until my favorite season of all.

6. What is this poem **mostly about?**
    A. playing baseball
    B. leaves falling
    C. cold winters
    D. a favorite season

7. Read this stanza from the poem.

    The leaves are colorful

    They always make me smile.

    The only problem is

    That they only stay for a while.

    The author **most likely**
    A. wishes the colors would stay longer.
    B. does not like the colors of the fall leaves.
    C. is happy that the season is short.
    D. is glad when fall is over.

8. According to this poem, the author **most likely**
    A. hates the snow.
    B. likes the summer.
    C. likes to play baseball.
    D. skis in the winter.

Go On

9. Read the graphic organizer below.

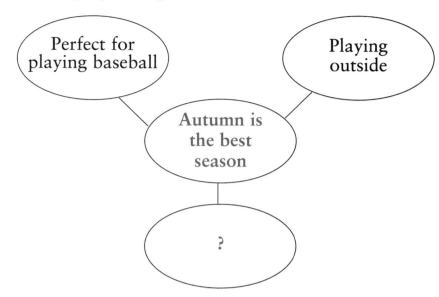

According to the poem, which detail best completes the graphic organizer?

A. The leaves are colorful.

B. The name is not important.

C. It is followed by winter.

D. People call it Fall.

10. This poem is best described as

A. fiction.

B. nonfiction.

C. a personal narrative.

D. a news article.

Directions:

Read the story "Grandma's Brownies" and answer questions 11–16.

Grandma's Brownies
By Janet Gallant

The smell of fresh baked brownies always reminds me of special weekends with my grandmother. She made the best homemade brownies! She taught me how to make her homemade brownies. Now I use the same recipe to make these delicious brownies for my family.

   If you love brownies like I do, you might want to follow this recipe and make these wonderful homemade brownies yourself.

   Before you start, be sure that you have everything you will need.

Supplies	Ingredients
Measuring cup	2 eggs
Measuring spoons	1 cup sugar
Spatula	½ cup flour
Electric mixer	2 squares baker's
Small saucepan	chocolate
8 × 8 baking pan	½ cup butter
Large mixing bowl	1 cup chopped walnuts
(large enough to	or chopped pecans
hold 4 cups of dry	Pinch of salt
ingredients)	

Go On

Before you start, be sure to ask a parent to help you!

Now you are ready to make the best homemade brownies.

First, melt the chocolate squares and the butter in a small saucepan. This is a step where an adult should help you. Let this melted mix cool while you do the next step.

Second, use the electric mixer and cream together the eggs, sugar, and flour. This step will be finished when the batter is smooth.

Third, add the cooled chocolate and butter mix to the batter you just made. Add the pinch of salt and mix everything together.

Next, use the spatula to pour the batter into the 8 × 8 baking pan. Put the brownies into an oven set at 350 degrees. Bake for about 18 minutes.

How will you know if the brownies are ready? Here's a test that an adult can do for you. Put a toothpick into the brownie near the edge of the pan. If the toothpick comes out clean, the homemade brownies are finished cooking.

When the brownies are cool, cut them into squares and share them with your family. Don't forget to breathe in the wonderful smell that has filled the kitchen. It will create a very special memory for you, too.

11. According to the author, the first thing you need to do to bake homemade brownies is
    A. cream together the eggs, sugar, and flour.
    B. test the brownies to see whether they are ready.
    C. be sure to have everything you will need.
    D. let them cool before you cut them.

12. Read this line from the story.

    Before you start, be sure to ask a parent to help you!

    The author **most likely** said this because
    A. she did not think children can bake brownies.
    B. she wants an adult to eat the brownies.
    C. she cooked with her grandmother.
    D. she wants to keep you safe near the oven.

13. The chart below shows the steps in making home-made brownies.

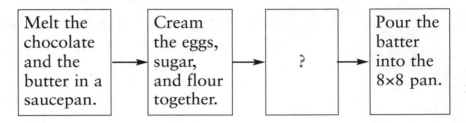

| Melt the chocolate and the butter in a saucepan. | → | Cream the eggs, sugar, and flour together. | → | ? | → | Pour the batter into the 8×8 pan. |

    Which sentence belongs in the empty box?
    A. Gather all the ingredients.
    B. Ask an adult for help.
    C. Add the chopped walnuts or pecans.
    D. Test the brownies to see if they are ready.

14. Read this line from the story.

    Add the pinch of salt and mix everything together.

    The word "pinch" **most likely** means
    A. a full cup.
    B. a teaspoon.
    C. the amount you can pinch between your fingers.
    D. the amount that will shake out of a salt shaker.

Go On

15. According to this story, which statement is an opinion?

  A. You will need a large mixing bowl.

  B. You can smell the brownies as they are baking.

  C. Grandma made the best homemade brownies.

  D. The brownies are ready when the toothpick comes out clean.

16. The author mostly likely wrote this story to

  A. give the reader a cooking lesson.

  B. share a special memory.

  C. tell the reader to cook with an adult.

  D. tell the reader the ingredients in brownies.

Directions:

Read the article called "Elephants" and answer questions 17–21.

Elephants
By Kate Gallant

What image do you see when you try to picture an elephant in your mind? Perhaps you see a large animal with a long trunk, big ears, and big feet. Elephants are all that and more.

Elephants are the largest animals on land. They are also one of the smartest. Elephants can also be called gentle. You can see an elephant at a zoo, in a circus, or in the wild in Africa, India, or Asia.

If you see an elephant in a circus, you will see why people call them gentle and smart. Circus elephants learn to perform many clever tricks. They are also gentle enough to let someone ride high on their backs as they perform circus tricks.

Most circus elephants are from India. They are large, but they are not the largest elephants in the world. The largest elephants are from Africa. The African elephant grows to 9 feet tall. The largest African elephant stands 12 feet tall. It lives in the wilds of Africa. African elephants are not only taller than other elephants but also have the largest ears.

The elephant is also known for its nose, called a trunk. It is the largest nose of any animal. Elephants use their large trunks in many ways. The elephant uses its trunk to eat. The trunk can pick up leaves off the ground or reach high into tall trees and grab nice fresh leaves for the elephant to eat.

Elephants also use their trunks to drink. They suck up water in their trunks and then squirt the water into their mouths. They might even squirt the water on their backs to shoo away flies. An elephant's trunk is strong enough to move a heavy log and delicate enough to pick to up a tiny peanut. The elephant can use its trunk to place the peanut in its mouth almost the same way that you and I use our fingers.

An elephant also uses its trunk to show its gentle nature. Elephants greet each other with their trunks. They wrap their trunks together in a sign of greeting much like we might shake hands. A mother elephant can even use her trunk to "hug" her baby elephant.

Go On

17. This article is **mostly about**
  A. a circus animal.
  B. interesting facts about elephants.
  C. African elephants have big ears.
  D. circus elephants come from India.

18. The largest African elephant is
  A. 9 feet tall.
  B. 12 feet tall.
  C. 6 feet tall.
  D. 20 feet tall.

19. Use a detail from the article to complete the following web. Write the answer below.

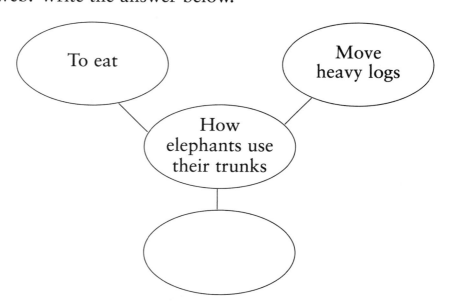

20. Read the chart below.

Places Where Elephants Live in the Wild
Africa
India
?

According to the article, which answer best completes the chart?

A. Asia

B. Canada

C. Japan

D. Mexico

21. Read this line from the article.

The elephant can also use its trunk to show its gentle nature.

In this sentence, the term "gentle nature" most likely means

A. quiet and small.

B. loud and mean.

C. soft and smooth.

D. kind and caring.

SESSION 2, DAY 2

BOOK 2: LISTENING AND WRITING

PART 1: LISTENING

Directions:

In this part of the test, you are going to listen to a story called "The Golfing Champions." Then you will answer some questions about the story. You will have 15 minutes to answer the questions after you have listened to the story two times. You will listen to the story twice. The first time you hear the story, listen carefully but do not take notes. As you listen to the story the second time, you may want to take notes. You may use these notes to answer the questions that follow. Your notes will NOT count toward your final score.

Notes

The Golfing Champions
By Emma Baker

My name is David. I am a middle child. I have two little sisters, Danielle and Sarah. They are twins. I have one big sister, too. Her name is Amy. She's old enough to drive. I love to play miniature golf. My dad and I are the champions at the Golden Golf Course.

You need to practice a lot to win a championship. But sometimes practicing is hard. Well, actually it's not the practicing that's hard. The hard part can be getting to the golf course! Some days that is harder than others! This is the story of one really hard practice!

"Mom," I said as I was quickly eating my breakfast, "I'm going to the miniature golf course to meet dad."

"Okay," said Mom. "Take Danielle and Sarah with you."

"Do I have…." I stopped. I knew the answer.

"I am busy, though. Who is driving you?" asked Mom.

"Amy," I said as I finished putting on my sneakers.

"WHAT?" said Amy, stomping out of her room. "I am not driving a bunch of little kids to the golf course. I am going to meet my friends at the China Town Restaurant to have lunch."

"But, Mom," I said. "I have to go to the golf course. Dad signed us up for the championship and this will be our last day for training before the championship. I have to go!"

"A-a-m-m-y-y," Mom said in a voice that told Amy she had no choice.

"Fine," yelled Amy. "I'll drive you. Let's go."

Now, maybe you are thinking my troubles ended there. Wrong. The championship match was the next day. Dad wanted the family to drive to the golf course together in the family van. It was time to go. Everyone was ready to go; everyone, that is, except Amy.

Go On

"Come on, let's go!" Dad and I yelled. "We need to go now."

"Wait, where is Amy?" Mom asked.

Just then, we all heard the water running in the shower. Amy was not even dressed yet!

"M-m-o-m-m," I said. "Make her hurry. We will be late. We can't be late. We can't win if we are late. Make her hurry. Please."

Mom went upstairs and talked to Amy. Five minutes later, we were on the road. We came to a sign that said Golden Golf Course.

"Wow, this is amazing." I said. "It's so cool!"

The teams were standing together, and it was time to start the game.

Six hours later, Dad and I were tied for first place. It was 72 to 72. Dad and I could win the match if we won this hole.

My dad shot first. He did great. Now it was up to me! I gripped my golf club. I got scared that we were going to lose. I looked over at the huge trophy. I heard my dad say, "You can make this shot."

Everyone yelled and cheered. I made it. Dad and I won the championship. Dad and I stood there with the trophy as my family gathered around. Mom, Danielle, Sarah, and … Amy. She said she wouldn't have missed this for the world!

22. According to David, who caused most of the problems in this story?

  A. David's twin sisters

  B. David's sister, Amy

  C. David

  D. The owner of the golf course.

23. Read this sentence from the story.

"WHAT?" said Amy stomping out of her room.

This sentence most likely means that:

A. Amy was happy to drive the children to the golf course.

B. Amy did not hear what David said.

C. Amy did not want to drive the children to the golf course.

D. Amy was surprised to hear what David said.

24. According to the information in this story, David was upset when his sister was in the shower because

A. it was his turn to use the shower.

B. Amy was using all the hot water.

C. Amy is late for everything.

D. he was afraid he would miss the championship.

25. The chart below shows what happens in the story. Complete the chart using details from the story.

WHAT HAPPENS IN THE STORY

The score is tied 72 to 72.

Dad makes a great shot.

David and his father win the golf championship.

Go On

26. How do you know that David is nervous about winning the championship? Use details from the story in your answer.

_____

_____

_____

_____

_____

_____

27. According to the information in this story, David said this practice was hard because

A. David did not like to practice.

B. David did not know how to play golf.

C. David was not sure his sister would drive him to the golf course.

D. David was afraid that he would not win the championship.

PART 2: WRITING

Directions:

Look at the paragraph. There are some mistakes in this paragraph in capital letters and punctuation. Let's correct the mistakes together. Draw a line through each part that has a mistake, and if a correction needs to be written, write it above the mistake.

New york had a big snowstorm today! It snowed for

six hours? the ground was covered with 10 inches of

snow. Too bad it was saturday. We missed out on a

snow day.

Now take a look at the corrections you should have made.

York
New ~~york~~ had a big snowstorm today! It snowed for
      hours. The
six ~~hours? the~~ ground was covered with 10 inches of
                                    Saturday
snow. Too bad it was ~~saturday.~~ We missed out on a

snow day.

Go On

Explanation:

Line 1 has one error. New York is a proper name. Both words in the name must begin with a capital letter.

Line 2 has two errors. *It snowed for six hours* is a statement and should end with a period and not a question mark. The next sentence must begin with a capital letter.

Line 3 has an error in capitalization. The first word in the sentence must begin with a capital letter.

Note: The first sentence ends with a punctuation mark. The author placed it there to show emotion. If you change the exclamation point to a period, it would not count as a mistake.

28. Here is a paragraph a student wrote about playing with a friend. The paragraph has some mistakes in capital letters and punctuation. Some sentences may have no mistakes. There are <u>no</u> mistakes in spelling.

Read the paragraph, and find the mistakes. Draw a line through each mistake in the paragraph. Then write the correction above it.

I am going to meet my friend jane after school today.

we are going shopping to buy her a new bicycle? Mrs.

Smith will help Jane learn how to ride her new bicy-

cle. Jane and i will ride our bikes to school.

Glossary

The words in this glossary are important words that will help you understand the language on the ELA tests. You may know many of these words already. Some may be new to you.

Many of the words on this list are explained in the guided test practices in this book. The practice pages refer you to this list for more detailed information. Review the words on this list before you begin the practice tests.

Adjective—describes a noun or a pronoun by telling more about it.

> *Example:* "Mom tried to ride down the steep hill."
> The word steep tells you more about the hill. The adjective can help you form a detailed picture in your mind. This picture will help you see what the author wants you to see.

Adjectives can help you understand the details of the text.

Antonyms—words that have meanings that are almost opposite.

> *Examples:* happy/sad
> hot/cold

Article—a written text, usually nonfiction.

Author's meaning—the information or point of view the author wants the reader to understand.

Character—the people and animals in a story. The characters can be a very important part of the story. Pay attention to their names and how they look and act.

The characters can be important because they can help the reader understand the story

- by the words they say out loud or in their thoughts
- by the way they act as events happen in the story
- by the way they change as the plot continues
- by the way they act and talk to each other.

Example: In the story "The Mermaids," Maggie's sister brought a camera when she went to the beach. Her *thoughts* told you that she did not believe in mermaids, but her *actions* showed that part of her *did* believe her sister was telling the truth.

Compare—to think about how two or more things are the same or different. When someone reads, they might compare two characters in the story. A reader can also think about how they would feel in the same situation and compare their thoughts and feelings with the way the character thinks and feels. This can help the reader understand the story.

Example: In the poem "Autumn," the author describes how he feels about the season. The reader might think about their feelings about fall and compare those to the feelings that the author is describing in the poem.

Conflict—a problem in the story. As you read or listen to a story, listen for the conflict. Is there a problem that a character has to solve? How is the problem solved?

Example: In the story "The Golfing Champions," David had to solve a problem. He needed a ride to the golf course and he needed the family to get to the golf course on time for the championship. As you listened to the story the first time, you learned that this story plot had a conflict. Amy was part of the problem, and

David had to find a solution. When you take notes, you can write down the details that will help you remember the important details.

Constructed response—an answer to a comprehension question that is written by an individual. The information needed to answer the question will be included in the passage read, but the reader must write the response in their own words.

Dialogue—the talking that takes place between characters in a story.

Event—an action or happening in a fiction or nonfiction text.

Fact—a thing known to be true.

> *Example:* The longest day of the year is called the summer solstice.

Fiction—writing that is made up or invented.

> *Examples:* fantasies, science fiction

"The Mermaids" is fiction. Mermaids are not real. This story was made up by the author.

Figurative language—words used by the author to create a special image in the mind of the reader. Sometimes the words do not mean what they seem to mean. Figurative language is often used to help the reader compare something they know to something that may be less familiar to them. Figurative language is used by the author to clarify a detail that is important in the story.

> *Example:* In the article "Seasons Change," the author writes "...night skies that never want to become dark." The skies cannot *think* about staying dark. The author wants the reader to understand that the sun stays up for so long that it seems *as if* the skies are trying to stay light on purpose.

Figures of speech—an author can use language in different ways to create strong images for the reader. Understanding figures of speech helps the reader understand the meaning the author wants them to understand.

Figures of speech include similes and metaphors.

Genre—a specific type of writing. (There is a chart that explains each genre.)

Graphic organizer—a form that organizes information and helps the reader understand information quickly. A graphic organizer can be used to help you understand what is read. A graphic organizer can also help a listener organize their notes as they listen to a story.

Examples: chart, diagram, picture, story map, web

Homophone—a word that sounds like another word but has a different meaning and spelling.

Examples: to, two, too
          there, they're, their
          see, sea

Metaphor—a figure of speech that compares two things that are not alike.

Example: "Kate is a fish in the water." Kate is not really a fish. The author compares her to a fish in the water to give the reader an image of a girl that is fast and natural in the water.

Moral—the lesson the story teaches the reader. You will find a moral in a tale or a fable.

Multiple choice—several possible answers to a question; only one choice is the correct answer.

Nonfiction—a text that is true. The writing contains true material about people, places, and events.

Note taking—writing the most important information and details from a text that is read or heard.

Noun—the name of a person, place, or thing.

Opinion—something that a person thinks, believes, or feels. An opinion is something that someone else can disagree with because they do not feel the same way.

Example: "She made the best homemade brownies." This is the opinion of the author.

Note: In the story "Grandma's Brownies," the character does say that her grandmother made the best brownies. It is written in the story, but it is the character's opinion. It is a personal feeling, not a fact.

Paragraph—a group of sentences that contain a main idea and details to support the main idea.

Passage—a piece of written work. The word "passage" is used on the ELA test. It refers to the story or article that the reader will read or has just finished reading.

Plot—the action in a story. A plot can include a conflict with a problem and a solution. The order in which events happen can also be an important element in the plot.

Point of view—the opinion, attitude, or belief of the author or the characters in a story.

Example: In the article "Computers," the author thinks computers are important. Everything that he wrote tells the reader that computers are a good thing to have.

If the author did not like computers, his point of view would be different. Then the article would tell you why computers are not good to have.

Pronoun—a word that is used in place of a noun.

Examples: I, you, he, she, we, they, them, someone

Purpose—the reason the author is writing the text.

Examples: the author may want to describe, explain, tell a story, or convince the reader to do or believe something.

Recall—to bring back from memory; to remember.

Selection—a short piece of writing such as a story or article.

Sensory detail—words included in a text to help the reader imagine the details the writer is describing. The details help the reader to hear, see, taste, smell, or feel what the author is describing.

Examples: The leaves are colorful.
The crowd cheered.
We drove through the streets so crowded with cars, all horns would constantly blow.

Sequence of events—the order in which things happen in a text.

Setting—where and when a story takes place.
Understanding the setting can help the reader:
create an image of the story in their mind
understand when the story takes place—past, present, or in the future
understand the changes that occur in the story

Simile—words that compare two unlike things. A simile uses the word "like" or "as" to help the reader understand the author's point of view and understand the author's intended meaning.

Example: Giraffes as tall as a cloud.

Stanza—the arrangement of lines in a poem.

Story—a piece of writing that tells about something that happened. A story can be fiction (made up) or nonfiction (real).

Story elements—important parts of a story. A reader uses the story elements to help them understand the story.

Examples: genre, title, characters, setting, point of view, plot, conflict

Summarize—to write or recall the most important elements and details of a text that is read or heard.

Supporting details—additional information that helps the reader understand or visualize the main idea. The supporting details are used to develop the story, explain the author's point of view, and provide additional information for the reader.

Synomyms—two words that have almost the same meaning.

Examples: Giant/huge
Frigid/freezing

Theme—the main idea or meaning of a text.

Text—a word used to describe a variety of styles of writing. The word "text" is used on the ELA test to refer to the story or article included in the test.

Topic sentence—The sentence that states the main idea of a paragraph.

Verb—a word that shows the action in a sentence.

HELPING YOUR CHILD DRAW CONCLUSIONS AND MAKE INFERENCES

When an author writes fiction or nonfiction, they do not describe every detail needed to understand the text. That could make for some very long and boring reading. Instead, the author provides just enough information and description to keep the reader interested. At the same time, the author gives the reader clues to help them make inferences and draw conclusions about the deeper meaning of the text.

An author may use figurative language to help the reader create an accurate image in their mind as they read the written text. Rich and colorful language adds a special quality to writing. The reader has to think about what the author says and think about the author's intended meaning.

The samples below model the thinking process used when reading figurative language. The stories are included in this practice book.

"Winter Vacation"

The author wrote:

Mom was remembering Dad rolling down the hill next to her. "Let's have a different kind of fun this vacation."

The author wanted the reader to understand:

The vacation last year *was* fun, but dad could have been hurt when he fell. So, this year she wants to have a vacation that does not include someone falling hard enough to get hurt.

"Computers"

The author wrote:

If you have ever wondered about computers, then you are going to enjoy this article.

The author wanted the reader to understand:

I know a lot of interesting facts about computers. Read the article to learn them.

"Elephants"

The author wrote:

Elephants are all that and more.

The author wanted the reader to understand:

All of the information you have read so far is true, but there are also more interesting things to think about when you think about elephants. So, keep reading to find out more.

"The Golfing Champions"

The author wrote:

"A-a-m-m-y," Mom said in a voice that told Amy she had no choice.

The author wanted the reader to understand:

Amy's mother meant what she said. There would be no arguing. Amy knew she had to drive her brother and sisters to the golf course.

"Sight to See"

The author wrote:

"Yes." her father agreed, "It is all about where you happen to be standing."

The author wanted the reader to understand:

An important detail in this story is the perception of size experienced by the main character, Cameron. When Cameron looked down, the people below looked small. Her father's words help the reader understand that no one changes their size, it just looks that way depending on where you are standing. When Cameron stands on the ground looking up, she knows that she looks very small to the people on the top of the building.

The last example demonstrates just how many words the author would have to write if the reader did not draw their own conclusions about the meaning of the story from the words the author uses.

Remember, good readers ask questions while they read. These questions can help them draw conclusions about the meaning of the text.

SCORING RUBRICS

The constructed-response questions and the editing paragraph will be scored using a scoring rubric.

A scoring rubric guides the evaluation of a written response. The Grade 3 ELA Test uses a 2-point scoring rubric to evaluate each constructed response, and a 3-point scoring rubric for the editing paragraph. Understanding the quality of each score point may help you understand the ELA test scoring process.

The rubrics below are the state ELA scoring rubrics. Further information can be found on the New York State Education Department website: *www.emsc.nysed.gov/ciai/ela*

CONSTRUCTED-RESPONSE 2-POINT SCORING RUBRIC

2 points   The response is accurate and complete, and it fulfills all the requirements of the task. Necessary support and/or examples are included, and the information given is clearly text-based. Any extensions beyond the text are relevant to the task.

1 point   The response includes some correct information but may be too general or overly specific. Some of the support and/or examples may be incomplete or omitted.

0 points   The response is inaccurate, confused, and/or irrelevant, or the student failed to respond to the task.

A summary of the scoring rubric is:

2	• Accurate and complete
	• Examples from the text are included
	• Response is based on the information from the text
1	• Contains *some* correct information
	• *Some* examples from the text are included
	• *Some* of the response is based on information from the text
0	• The response is *inaccurate*
	• The response *does not* respond to the question

Read the short story below. Read the constructed-response question. Read the constructed responses at each score point. Notice the difference between the three levels of response.

When I was a young girl, I enjoyed the family gatherings at my cousin's house. Lois lived in Hauppauge, New York. Her father had a house with a 5-acre backyard. That is a lot of backyard. Most of the property was covered by tall trees. On a windy day, you could hear the leaves brushing together as the wind whistled through the branches. I loved to visit in September when the leaves were rich with the colors of fall.

On special days, my cousin Nick would join the family gathering. Nick would bring along his dog. This was not your ordinary dog. This was a huge, furry, playful St. Bernard named Moose. His name described him perfectly. Moose was a moose!

In the evening, after a huge dinner, my cousin Michael would play the accordion and everyone would sing. Michael was an excellent accordion player. The music he made was wonderful. The love in our voices blended together to create an awesome sound. We all had a wonderful time.

Family gatherings were special events in my childhood. My father is one of 13 children. That means I had 12 uncles and 12 aunts. Each aunt and uncle had 2 or 3 children. So, my family gatherings usually included more than 50 people. When I stop and remember those wonderful days, I can smell the wonderful food and hear Moose barking. The best memory is the sound of the music that Michael played late into the night.

Constructed-response question:

How do you know the author of this story enjoyed her family gatherings? Use *details* from the story in your answer.

2	• Accurate and complete
	• Examples from the text are included
	• Response is based on the information from the text

The author enjoyed her family gatherings. She liked to visit her cousin in September to see the colorful leaves. She liked the sound of the wind in the trees. The author said that family gatherings were special events in her childhood. She enjoyed those special times.

This response is a *complete and accurate response*. The topic sentence restates the question. The paragraph *includes* examples that are the *details from the story*. The paragraph has a conclusion. This is an accurate and complete response.

1	• Contains *some* correct information
	• *Some* examples from the text are included
	• *Some* of the response is based on information from the text
	The author said she liked to go to her family gatherings.
	This response has *some correct information*, but it is very general. The response includes only one detail from the text.
0	• The response is *inaccurate*
	• The response *does not* respond to the question
	The author liked Moose.
	This response *does not* explain why the author liked her family gatherings.

To construct a complete response, it is important to include details from the text. Return to the story or look at your notes for details to include in your response.

EDITING TASK 3-POINT RUBRIC

3 points	No more than one error, either introduced or not corrected, remains after the student has corrected the paragraph.
2 points	Two errors, either introduced or not corrected, remain after the student has corrected the paragraph.
1 point	Three errors, either introduced or not corrected, remain after the student has corrected the paragraph.
0 points	Four or more errors, either introduced or not corrected, remain after the student has corrected the paragraph.

Here is a sample editing paragraph. The errors are marked in bold print. The corrections made are written above. The comments to explain the scoring are in blue.

3	
	I Baseball season starts in two weeks. ~~i~~ am going to try out for weeks. the local team. My father and I practiced for three ~~weeks?~~ Tigers. This I am ready to be a catcher for the ~~tigers.~~ ~~this~~ may be the best summer of my life. All mistakes were identified and corrected.

2	I
	Baseball season starts in two weeks. ~~i~~ am going to try out
	
	Father weeks.
	for the local team. My ~~father~~ and I practiced for three ~~weeks?~~
	
	This
	I am ready to be a catcher for the tigers. ~~this~~ may be
	
	life!
	the best summer of my ~~life.~~
	
	This paragraph has two errors.
	    Line 2: "father" should not have a capital letter. It is not a
	        proper name (introduced error).
	    Line 3: "Tigers" is the name of the team and should have a
	        capital letter (error not corrected).
	    Line 4: A period or an exclamation point is correct punctuation.
	        This change does not count as an error.

1	I Baseball season starts in two weeks. ḭ am going to try out for the local team. My father and I practiced for three weeks? I am ready to be a catcher for the tigers. this may be the best summer of my life. This paragraph has three errors remaining.
0	I Baseball season starts in two weeks. ḭ am going to try out Father for the local team. My ~~father~~ and I practiced for three weeks? I am ready to be a catcher for the tigers. this may be the best summer of my life. This paragraph has four errors. Three errors are not identified and corrected. One error is introduced.

Read the editing paragraph more than once before you begin to make corrections. Look for capital letters at the beginning of each sentence. Look at the punctuation at the end of each sentence. Look for proper names that need to have a capital. Remember, the editing paragraphs are short and contain very few sentences. You should not expect to find a large number of errors to correct.

Appendix 4

PARENT REPORT CARD

T he local school district will mail a copy of the Parent Report developed by the New York State Education Department to the student's parent or legal guardian. This report will explain the student's individual results. The report does not explain state or local school district results. The New York State Education Department suggests that parents and guardians refer to this report when talking to the child's teacher about the strength and needs of the child as measured by the state assessment test.

UNDERSTANDING YOUR CHILD'S SCORE AND PERFORMANCE LEVEL

The following is a brief summary of what is included on the report.

SCALE SCORE

The scale score is an estimate of achievement based on one test. Scale scores can be compared from year to year. A score of 650 indicates a minimum proficiency.

Therefore, if a student receives a scale score of 660 on the Grade 3 ELA Test, the student has met the state standard for grade 3. Further, if the student receives a 680 on the Grade 4 ELA test the following year, the student's skills are improving.

PERFORMANCE LEVEL

The performance level indicates how the child is meeting the New York State standards for English Language Arts. There are four levels of performance defined as follows:

Level 4: Meeting learning standards with distinction

Level 3: Meeting learning standards

Level 2: Partially meeting learning standards

Level 1: Not meeting learning standards.

STANDARD PERFORMANCE INDEX

A third score that is presented on the Parent Report is the Standard Performance Index (SPI). Translated simply, if the student receives a SPI of 55 in one standard, it is estimated that if given 100 questions measuring that particular standard, the student would be expected to answer 55 of the questions correctly. To determine if the student meets the expected level of proficiency for that standard, the student's SPI must fall within the target range for the standard. The target range is indicated on the Parent Report.

ACADEMIC SUPPORT

If a student receives a performance level of less than 3, the school district will provide Academic Intervention Services (AIS) to the student. These services are intended to provide the student an opportunity for academic achievement. Contact the local school district for information and for the services provided by the district.

For more information, visit the New York State Department of Education website: *www.NYSParents.com*.

NEW YORK STATE TESTING PROGRAM

THE NO CHILD LEFT BEHIND ACT

In 2001, the federal government passed an education initiative called The No Child Left Behind Act (NCLB). The purpose of NCLB is to ensure that all children have an opportunity to obtain a high-quality education. Improved student achievement is a key component of the No Child Left Behind Act. A goal of NCLB is for all students to be proficient in English and Mathematics by the school year 2013–2014.

State and local districts are accountable for student achievement in their schools. To measure student achievement and yearly progress, NCLB requires school districts to test all students in grades 3–8. The New York State ELA testing program is in response to NCLB and accountability for student achievement.

ADEQUATE YEARLY PROGRESS

Under NCLB, every state has to implement a system to measure the achievement level of all students in grades 3–8. The annual tests will ensure that all schools are making adequate yearly progress toward 100% proficiency for the year 2013–2014.

UNDERSTANDING THE SCHOOL DISTRICT'S TEST RESULTS

The results of the New York State ELA Test are reported to the public by subgroups. Individual student results are not reported to the public. School- and districtwide results are helpful to measure the effectiveness of a school's instructional program. The results are used to determine if the district has made adequate yearly progress.

For more information about NCLB, visit the U.S. Department of Education website: *http://www.ed.gov/nclb/landing.jhtml.*

Answer Key

TEST YOUR SKILLS
CHAPTER 1

Question	Answer	Explanation
1	A	*Use a detail from the text* The answer is stated in the first line of the poem.
2	B	*Connect details from the text / draw a conclusion* The diapers acting like a soft padding. Landing on something soft did not hurt the baby.
3	D	*Vocabulary / context clues / draw conclusion* The poem tells you that the baby falls a lot while she is learning to walk. You can draw the conclusion that the baby loses her balance and falls.
4	C	*Make a connection to the character / draw a conclusion* The person telling the story tells you that he or she want to play with his or her baby sister. But, the story teller wants to go outside and run. The baby sister cannot run yet, so the story teller runs with Pete instead.

153

CHAPTER 2

Question	Answer	Explanation
1	CR	*Make a connection to the character / draw a conclusion* A complete answer would demonstrate an understanding that: • the baby is just learning to walk. • the baby takes a few steps and falls. • the baby needs more time to become *steady* on her feet. • then she can play outside.
2	CR	*Vocabulary / context clues / draw conclusion* A complete answer would demonstrate an understanding that: • the baby's diaper is thick and soft. • when the baby fell she landed on her diaper. • the soft diaper protected the baby; she did not get hurt.

CHAPTER 3

Question	Answer	Explanation
1	C	*Main idea* This story is *mostly about* a young girl who will sleep over at a friend's house for the very first time.
2	A	*Make a connection to the character / draw a conclusion* Sally's mother cares about her daughter. She knows that Sally has never been away from home all night. She is worried because she does not know if Sally will feel homesick.
3	D	*Use a detail right from the text* This information is stated in the story.
4	CR	*Use a detail right from the text* The missing items are: • a raccoon pillow named Rocky. • a sleeping pillow stuffed with feathers. You should have written these details in your notes. Including both parts of each answer would be a full and complete response.

5	CR	*Make a connection to the character / draw a conclusion* A complete response would demonstrate an understanding of the following: • Sally had never stayed away from home overnight. • Sally did not want to feel homesick. • Sally brought her three favorite things with her to make her feel at home in Jane's house.
6	C	*Vocabulary / context clues / main idea /draw conclusion* This is a story about a girl who sleeps away from home for the first time. Mom is worried that Sally will miss her family.

CHAPTER 4

It is a warm and sunny day ~~today?~~ today. I think ~~i~~ I will do

my homework outside. My homework is to read a

book about Michael ~~jordan~~ Jordan. I will bring out my new

~~Rocking~~ rocking chair. The sun will feel wonderful.

PRACTICE TEST 1

Question	Answer	Explanation
1	B	*Make a connection to the character / draw a conclusion* Cameron's father had seen the view before and knew it was something special to see.
2	C	*Make a connection to the character / draw a conclusion* Cameron would be surprised if she had never seen the view from the top of the Empire State Building.
3	A	*Use a detail right from the text* This is a detail from the story. The author uses the same words that are in the story.
4	D	*Author's purpose* This story was a personal narrative. The author is telling you about an experience she had. The other choices are details from the story, not the main idea.
5	C	*Use a detail right from the text* This is a detail from the article. The author uses the same words in the article.
6	A	*Connect details from the text* The author tells you that summer is sunny and you can expect warm days. You had to search for the sentence and connect the information together.

7	A	*Figurative language* The author tells you that the sun stays up longer in the summer. You have to connect the cause (more sunlight) to the effect (the skies do not want to get dark).
8	C	*Use a detail from the text* You had to search the details stated in the text to find the one statement that was stated by the author.
9	B	*Author's purpose* This article was written to provide facts about the summer solstice.
10	D	*Main idea* The main idea of this poem is that someone is trying to imagine what might be found behind a locked attic door.
11	B	*Sequence of events* Use details from the poem. Think about what happened *just before* the door is discovered to be locked.
12	CR	*Use a detail right from the text* Place *one* of the items imagined in each of these two sentences: a key to the city; a suit of armor; a king's golden crown; a map to a treasure; a chest filled with ancient treasures; jewels worth a million dollars. 1. *The author imagined that a _____ _____ could be a lost attic treasure.* 2. *The author imagined that a _____ _____ could be a lost attic treasure.*

13	B	*Use a detail right from the text* The author tells you what they would do if they found jewels worth a million dollars.
14	D	*Main idea* This is a poem about someone using their imagination.
15	A	*Vocabulary and context clues* A person who uses their imagination would be described as imaginative.
16	C	*Use a detail right from the text* The author tells you the answer in the article, but you had to carefully decide *which* detail belongs in this chart.
17	A	*Use a detail right from the text* The author told you the answer in the article, but you had to search the text for the correct detail.
18	B	*Vocabulary and context clues* You had to know that variety means different kinds (think about a time you have heard that word before—a *variety* of flavors, a *variety* of shapes) and then think about the main idea of this text, which is playing the cello. Musical pieces would be songs.
19	B	*Fact or opinion* An opinion is something you cannot prove to be true and you can agree or disagree with the statement. Joy is an emotion. You can disagree with how someone feels about cello music.

20	D	*Make a connection to the character / draw a conclusion* In this case, the character is the author. The author stated that cello music can bring people joy.
21	A	*Use details from the text / draw a conclusion / vocabulary* Advice is something you give to try to help someone. The author is trying to help you learn to play the cello.
22	C	*Use a detail right from the text* The author uses the word for this answer in the story. It is an important detail that should be in your notes.
23	D	*Figurative language* Use the main idea of this story to help you understand that Maggie turned to look at something.
24	B	*Make a connection to the character and vocabulary* Maggie saw the mermaids. She knew she was not alone and knew her sister did not make the noise. She would be confused at this unexpected sight.

25	CR	*Use details from the text / draw a conclusion*

A complete answer would include some of the following details:

- The mermaids saw that Maggie's sister had a camera.
- If she took their picture, she might show it to other people.
- The mermaid king did not want people to know mermaids really do exist.
- The mermaids were told to stay away from people.
- The mermaids did not think Maggie's sister would keep their secret.

26	CR	*Sequence of events*

Think about the order of events in the story. A correct response includes any of the details below in the correct order.

- The mermaids introduce themselves to Maggie.
- The three swim together.
- They stop when they hear the school bell.
- The mermaids promise to come back the next day.
- The mermaids come back but stay away because Maggie's sister has a camera.
- They talk to Maggie after her sister leaves.
- They explain they cannot trust someone with a camera to keep their secret.

27	A	*Author's purpose / genre*
		Mermaids are not real. This must be a fantasy.

28	I
	Summer is my favorite time of year. ~~i~~ can swim in my
	
	                                                Friday
	backyard pool. I plan a sleepover party every ~~friday~~ night.
	                                                     We
	My friends come over and we swim until it gets dark. ~~we~~
	
	end the night with a pizza party. Do you like summer and
	                parties?
	sleepover ~~parties.~~

PRACTICE TEST 2

Question	Answer	Explanation
1	A	*Use a detail right from the text* This is a detail question. The author uses this word in the text.
2	C	*Use a detail right from the text* This is a detail question. The author uses this word in the text.
3	D	*Vocabulary and context clues* The author told you that these nanobots may go inside the body. This should help you make a connection to the words "microscope" and "microscopic."
4	C	*Author's purpose* This is an informational text. The author's purpose is to teach you new information.
5	B	*Fact or opinion* An **opinion** is something you cannot prove to be true. You can disagree with this statement because it is a personal opinion.
6	D	*Main idea* The main idea of this poem is a favorite season. The rest of the choices are details to explain why it is the author's favorite season.

7	A	*Make a connection to the character / draw a conclusion*
		The author likes the colors and *wishes they would stay longer.*
8	C	*Draw a conclusion using details from the text*
		The author tells the reader that baseball is something that he likes. The author does not make the other statements in the poem.
9	A	*Use details from the text /draw a conclusion*
		The author tells the reader that the *colorful leaves* are one reason that autumn is the best season of all.
10	C	*Author's purpose*
		The author wrote this poem to share his personal feelings about autumn.
11	C	*Use a detail from the text*
		This statement is a detail right from the text. The author uses the same words in the story.
12	D	*Use details from the text / draw a conclusion*
		You need to think about the heat of the oven and the injury that could happen if a child was not careful. An adult should be near to keep a child safe.
13	C	*Sequence of events*
		Use details from the story. Look back to see what happens just before the batter is poured into the pan.

14	C	*Use details from the text / draw a conclusion / context clue* The word "pinch" should help you answer this question.
15	C	*Fact or opinion* An opinion is something you cannot prove to be true. You can disagree with this statement because it is a personal opinion.
16	B	*Author's purpose* This story is a personal narrative. The author wanted to share a special memory with the reader.
17	B	*Author's purpose / main idea* This is an information text. The author wrote this article to tell the reader interesting facts about elephants. The other choices are details to support the main idea.
18	B	*Detail from the text* The author tells the reader this information in the article.
19	CR	*Detail from the text* Any *one* of the following would be correct: • Drink • Shoo away flies • Greet one another • Hug their baby

20	A	*Detail from the text* The author tells the reader this information in the article.
21	D	*Vocabulary and context clues / draw a conclusion using details from the text* Think about what the author has said about elephants and how they greet one another. Also, think about how a mother acts with her baby. The author gives the reader clues to answer this question.
22	B	*Use details from the text / draw a conclusion* David explains that his sister did not want to take him to practice *and* almost made him late for the championship. David thinks she caused the problems in this story.
23	C	*Use details from the text / draw a conclusion* The author uses the character's emotion to help you understand how she feels. The character also states that she does not want to drive a bunch of little kids to the golf course.
24	D	*Use details from the story / draw a conclusion / character's feelings* David's father wanted everyone to drive together in the van; it was getting late and Amy was not ready.

25	CR	*Sequence of events* **What happens *after* Dad made a good shot *and before* David and his father won the championship?** Any one of the following choices would be correct: • David is nervous. • David looks at the trophy. • Dad says, "You can make this shot." • David makes the shot. • Everyone cheers.
26	CR	*Use details from the text / draw conclusion / character's feelings* A sentence or a paragraph that describes any one of the following ideas is correct: • David insists he has to practice to win and is worried that his sister will not take him to practice. • David is worried when his sister is not ready to leave on time. He is afraid he will miss the championship and not have a chance to win. • When the score was tied, David knows he has to hit a good shot to win. He grips the club before his shot. • David looks at the trophy and gets nervous. He feels better after he hears his father tell him he believes that David can make the shot.

27	C	*Main idea / use details from the text / draw conclusion*
		This story is about a young boy who wants to win a golf championship. He knows he has practiced. In this story, he tells about a time when the hardest part was getting someone to drive him to the golf course.

28		

                                           Jane   We

I am going to meet my friend ~~jane~~ after school today. ~~we~~

                                                        bicycle.

are going shopping to buy her a new ~~bicycle?~~ Mrs. Smith

ill help Jane learn how to ride her new bicycle. Jane and

  I

~~i~~ will ride our bikes to school.

Index